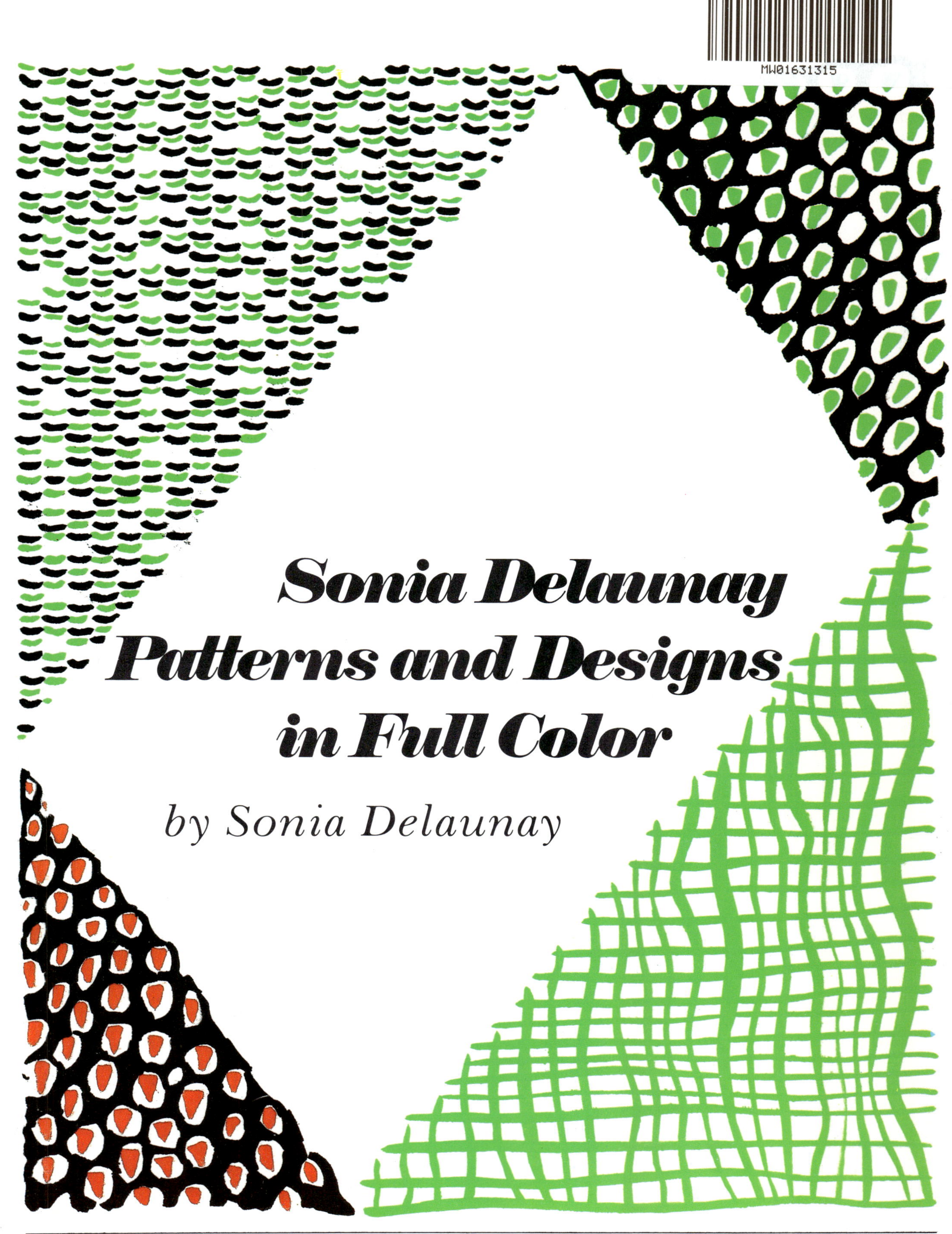

Sonia Delaunay Patterns and Designs in Full Color

by Sonia Delaunay

DOVER PUBLICATIONS, INC. • NEW YORK

Published in Canada by
General Publishing Company, Ltd.,
30 Lesmill Road, Don Mills, Toronto, Ontario.

Sonia Delaunay Patterns and Designs in Full Color,
first published by Dover Publications, Inc., in 1989,
reproduces all the plates from the two portfolios
described in the new Publisher's Note.

Manufactured in the United States of America
Dover Publications, Inc.
31 East 2nd Street
Mineola, N.Y. 11501

Library of Congress Cataloging-in-Publication Data

Delaunay, Sonia.
Sonia Delaunay patterns and designs in full color / by Sonia Delaunay.
p. cm.
ISBN 0-486-25975-7
1. Delaunay, Sonia—Themes, motives. 2. Design—France—History—20th century—Themes, motives. I. Title.
NK1535.D45A4 1989
745.4'4924—dc19 88-32715
CIP

Publisher's Note

SONIA TERK DELAUNAY was born in 1885 in the Ukraine and raised by an uncle in St. Petersburg. She studied art in Karlsruhe and, in 1906, came to Paris, where she was influenced by the works of Gauguin and van Gogh. In 1907 she met the painter Robert Delaunay (1885–1941), whom she married. She worked with him to develop the artistic principles that Guillaume Apollinaire, in 1912, named Orphism, a branch of Cubism that explored the full use of color in nonrepresentational forms. To this end, the Delaunays used what Robert termed "simultaneous contrasts," an approach to color inspired by *De la Loi du Contraste Simultané des Couleurs* (1839) by the famous chemist Michel-Eugène Chevreul. Colors in abstractions are allowed to play a unique role in establishing rhythm and mood. The Delaunays' work influenced the American Synchromist movement and some members of the Blauer Reiter group, including Paul Klee.

After a stay in the Iberian peninsula lasting from 1915 to 1920, the Delaunays returned to Paris. In 1937, the couple decorated the Air Pavilion and the Railway Pavilion at the Exposition Internationale in that city. Sonia Delaunay remained active after Robert's death, taking part in the establishment of the Salon des Réalités Nouvelles in 1947 and showing in many exhibitions. She died in 1979.

The plates in this volume are reproduced, in their original sequence, from two rare portfolios by Sonia Delaunay:

Sonia Delaunay: Ses Peintures, Ses Objets, Ses Tissus Simultanés, Ses Modes (pp. 1–20), was published by Librairie des Arts Décoratifs, Paris [1925?]. In addition to the plates by Delaunay, it contained poems by Joseph Delteil, Blaise Cendrars, Tristan Tzara and Philippe Soupault. In a preface, the painter and writer André Lhote makes the point that, with a few exceptions, the designs use no florals or other identifiable motif, the representation of nature being replaced by an interplay of abstract elements in a pure state. Forms are organized according to an easily perceived rhythm. (The Delaunays frequently thought of their art in musical terms.)

In this treatment, according to Lhote, everyday objects offer the artist the greatest challenge. In fact, Sonia Delaunay devoted her talents to all sorts of designs, from furniture and pottery to bookbindings and clothing. Her fashions were much in demand, not so much for originality of silhouette or construction as for inventiveness of patterning and use of fabric. Lhote says of these designs: "In an epoch when fashion sometimes so indiscreetly unveils the form, it is necessary that the bit of fabric used to cover it be decorated in the most abstract manner, so that the eye is for an instant attracted by the figures different from those born in intimacy." (Translation by H. C. Perleberg.)

Compositions, Couleurs, Idées (pp. 21–60) was published by Editions d'Art Charles Moreau, Paris [1930?]. The plates reveal Sonia Delaunay's further explorations with abstraction, playing color against color and form against form.

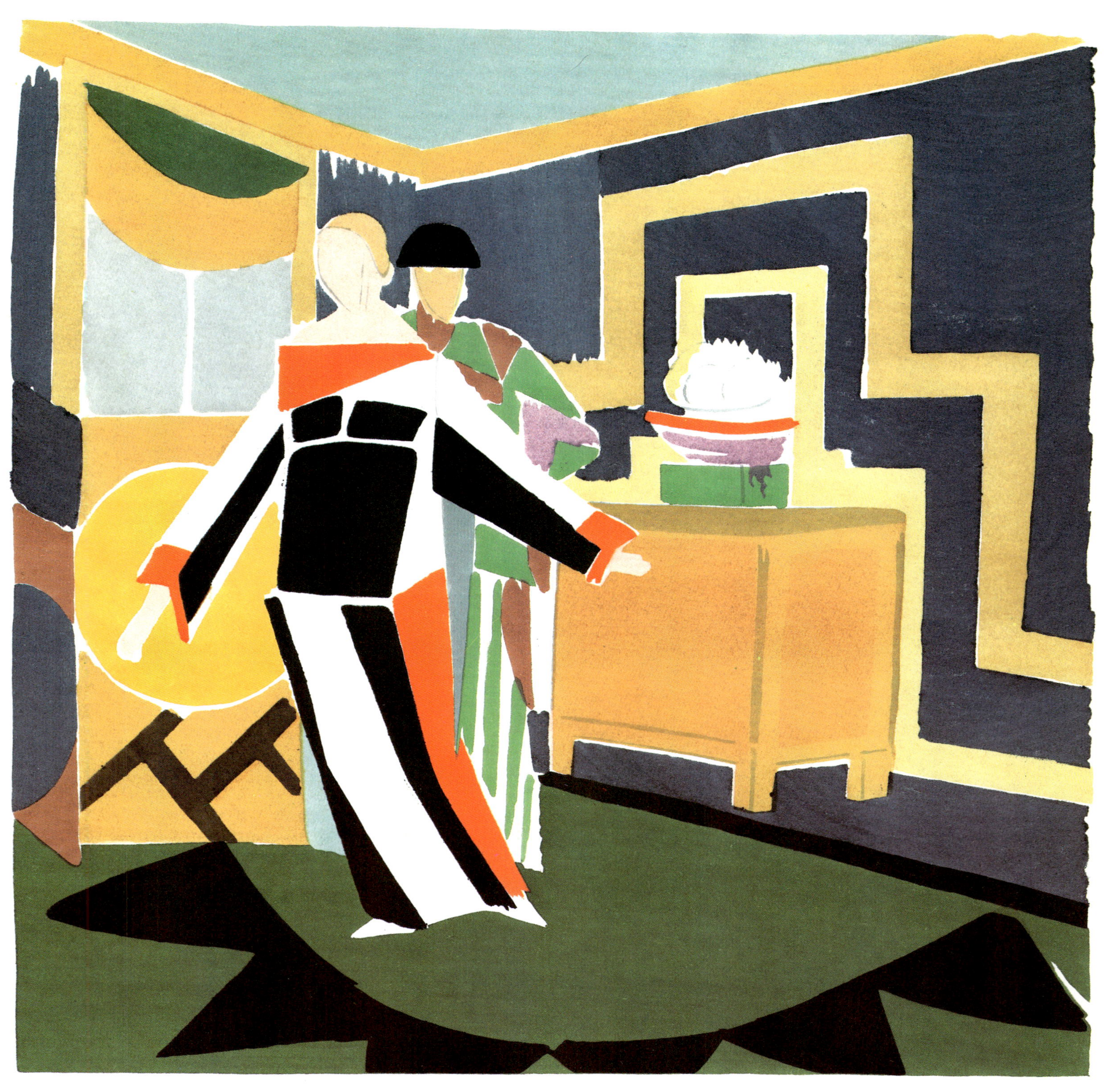

1923

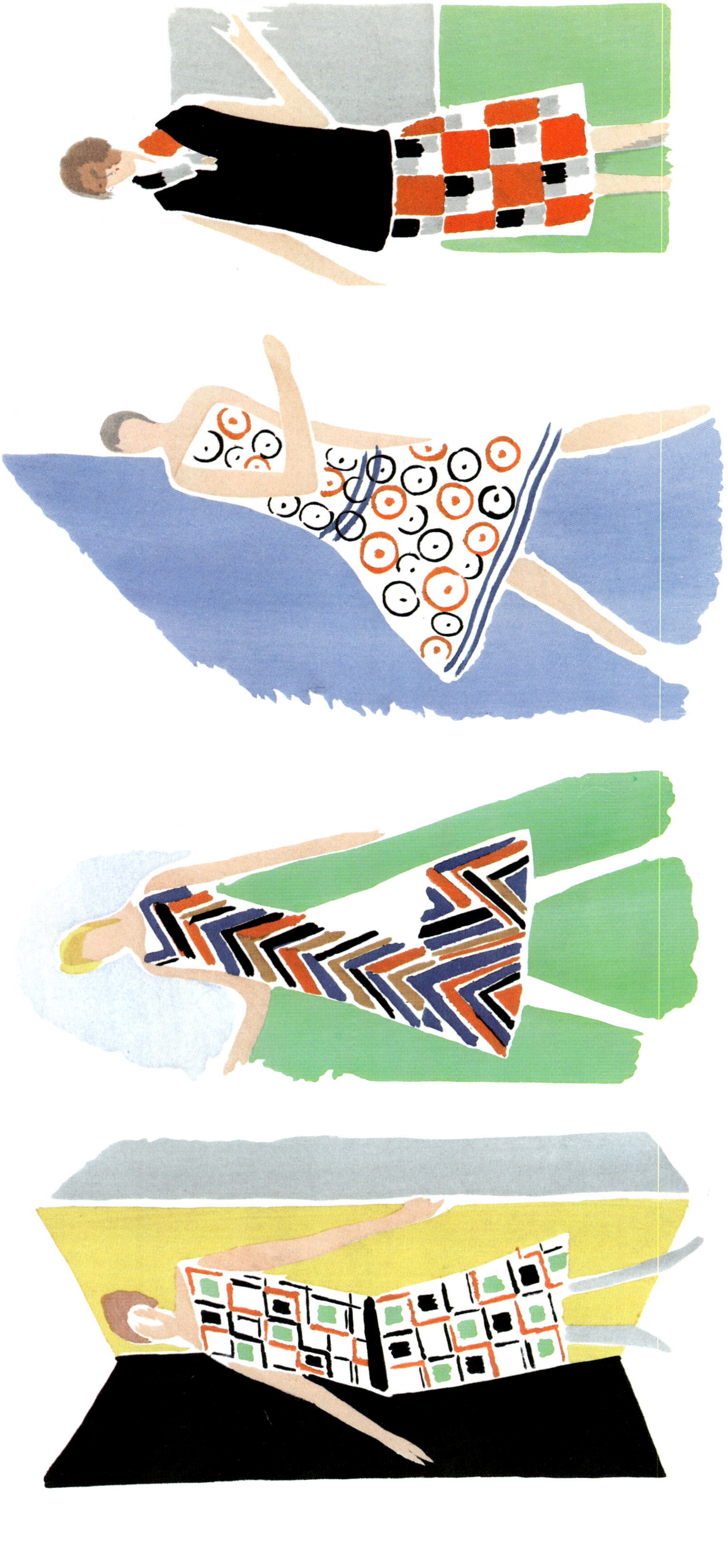

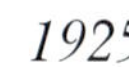

1925

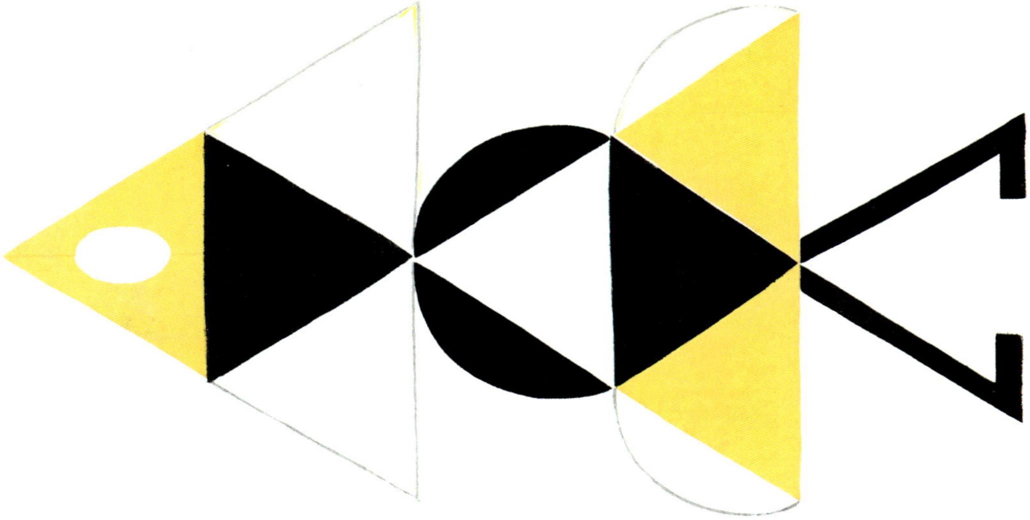

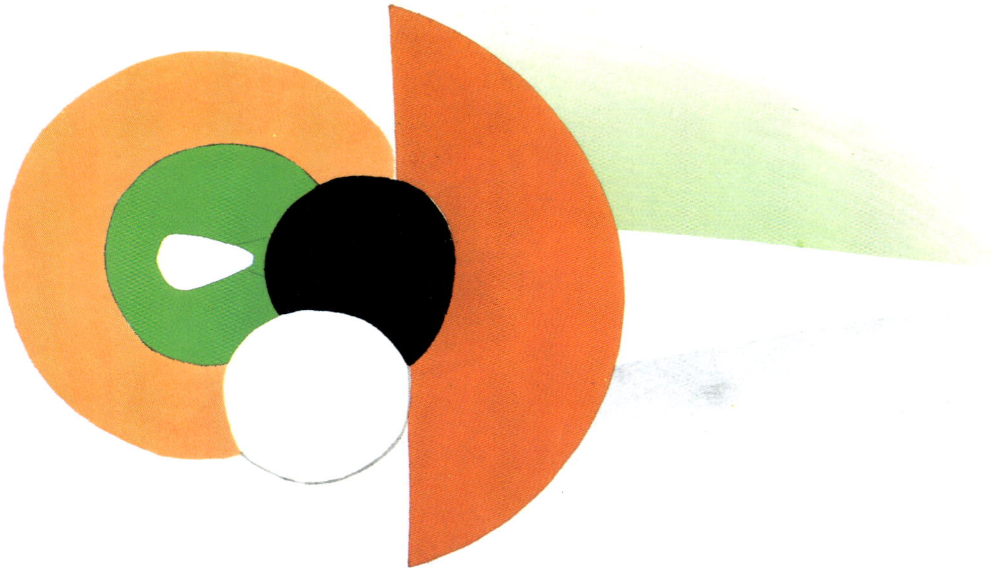

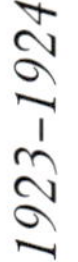

1923–1924

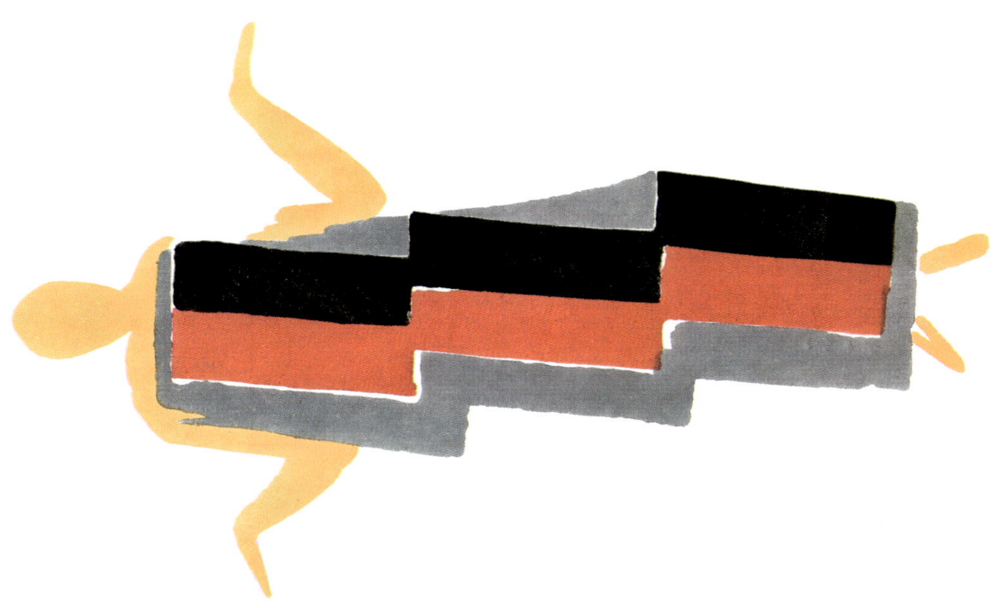

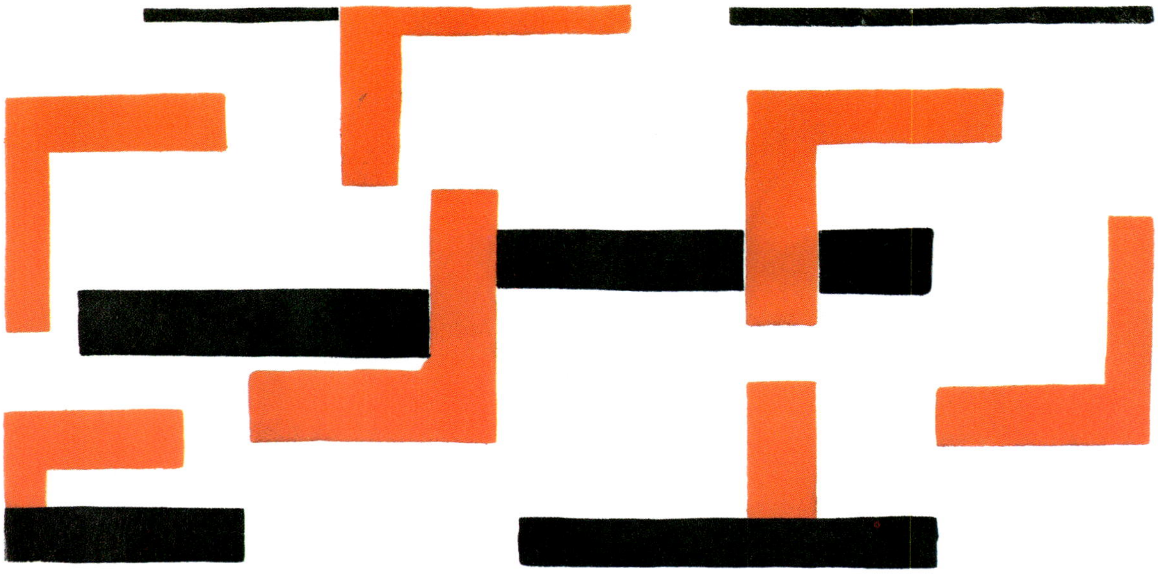

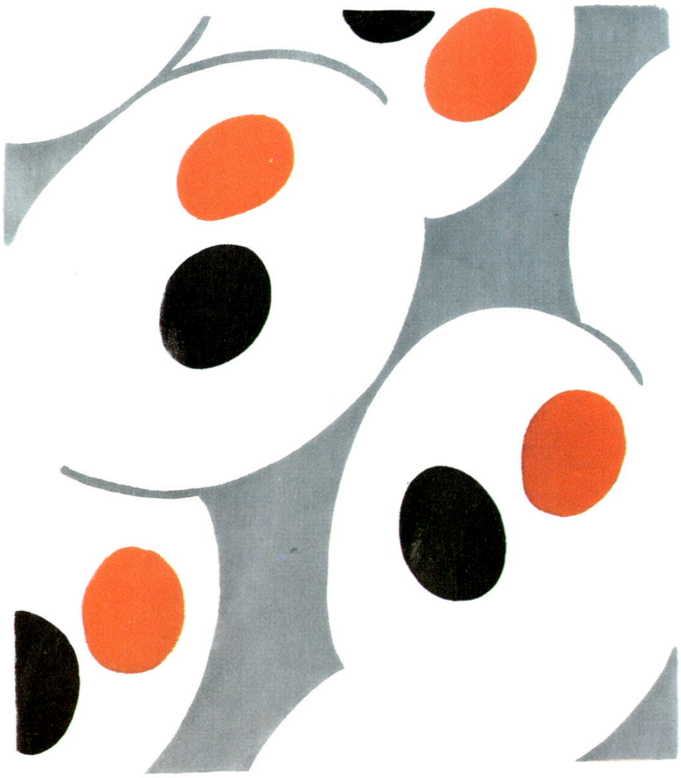

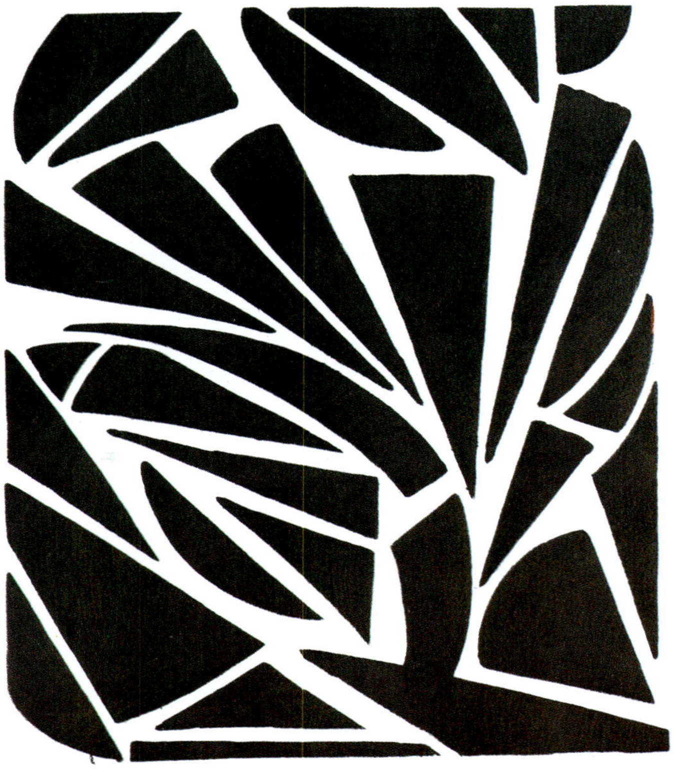

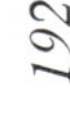

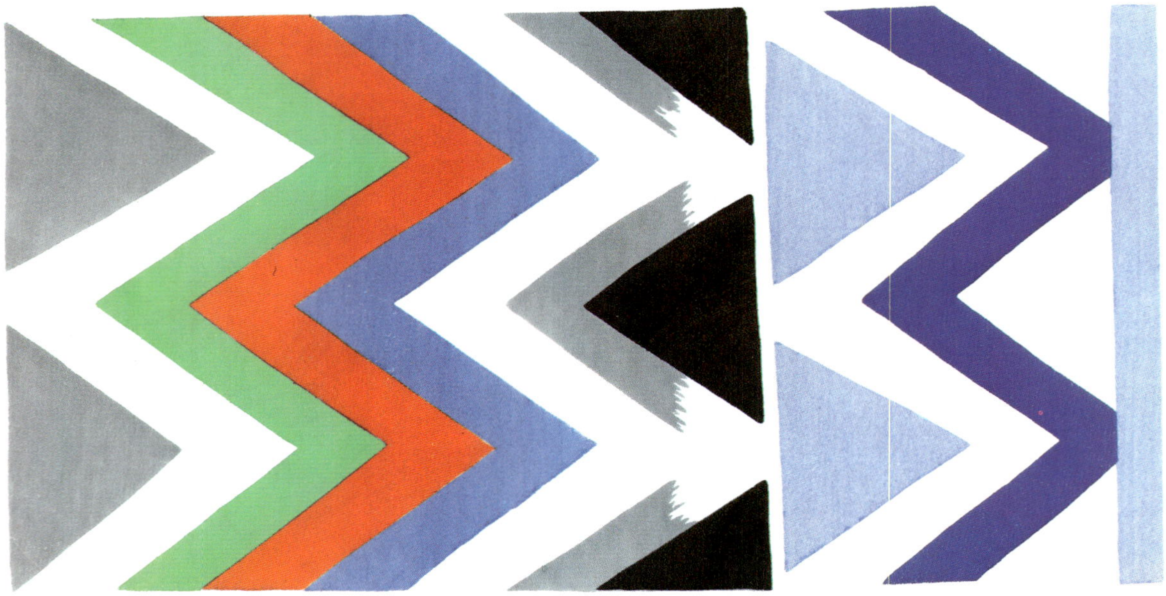

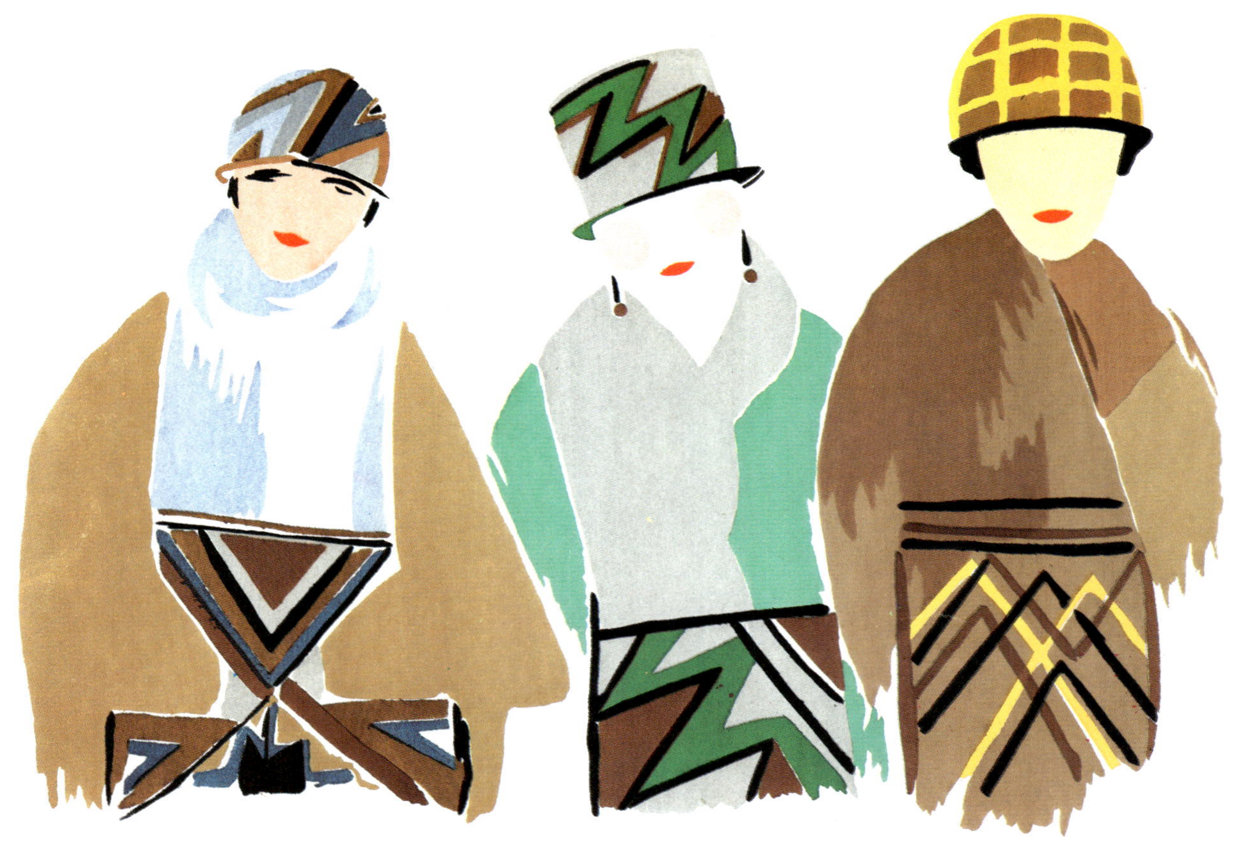

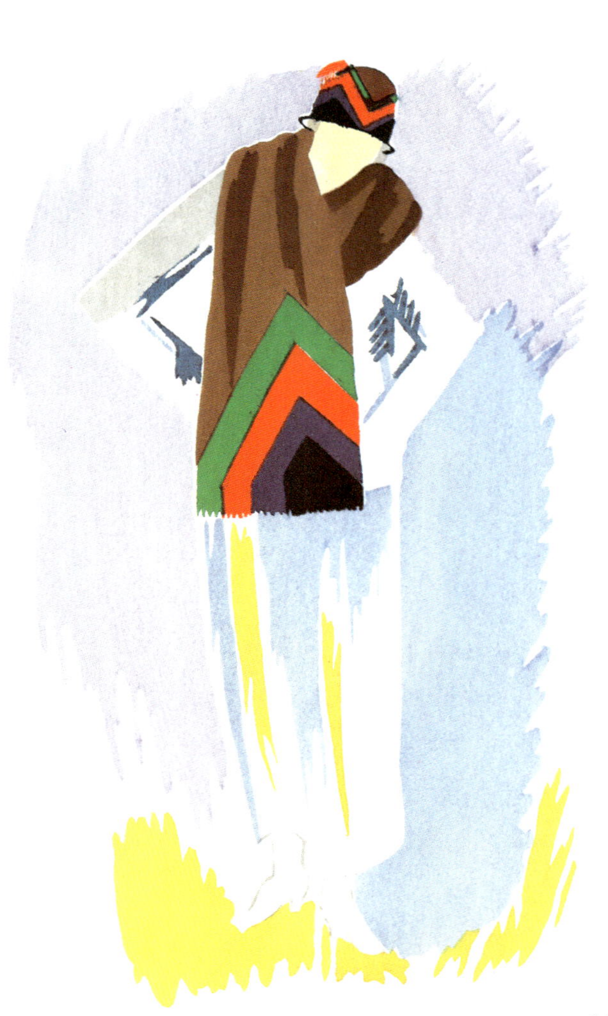

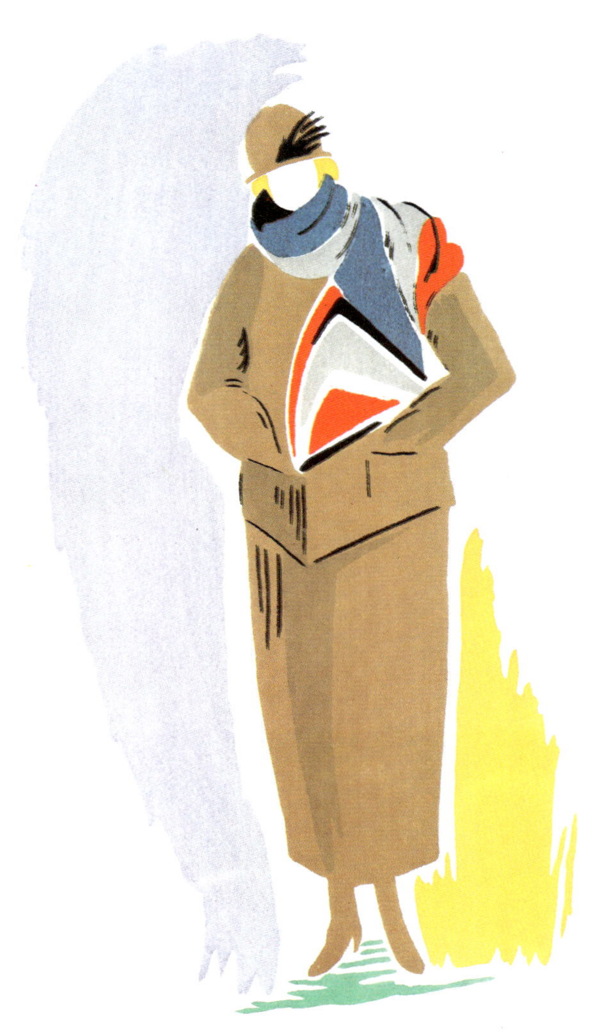

1922–1923

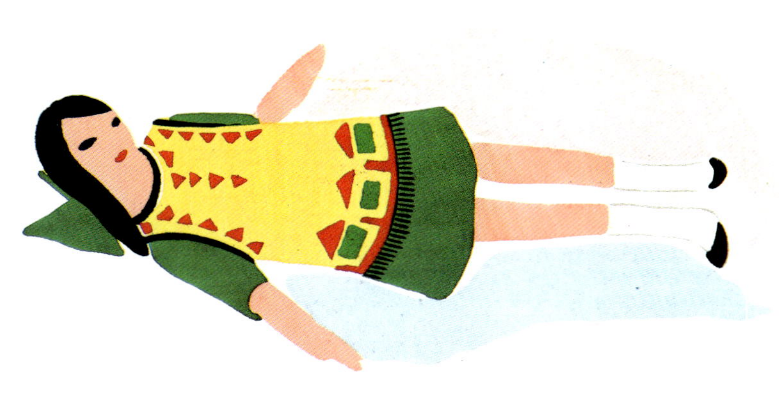

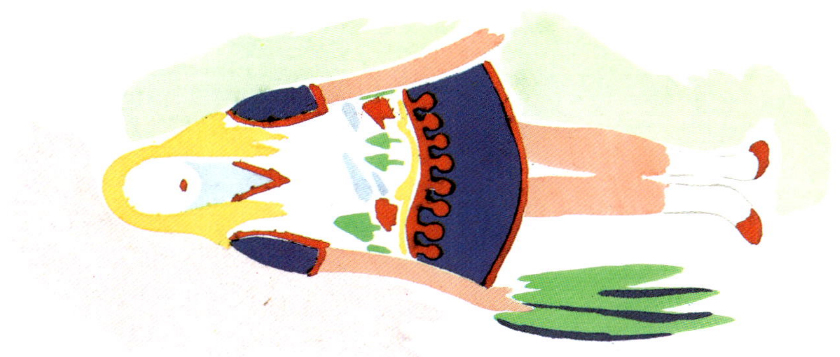

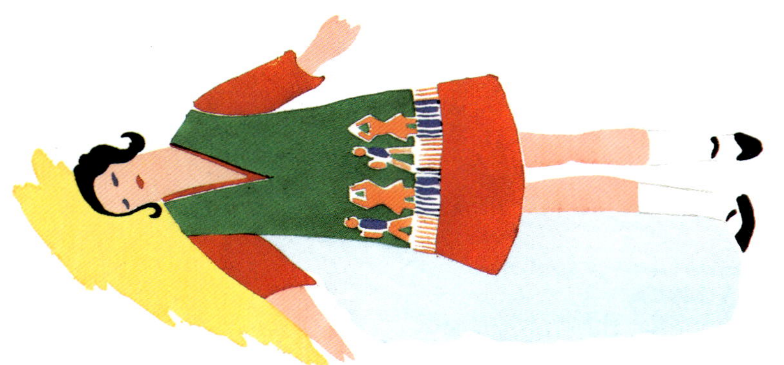

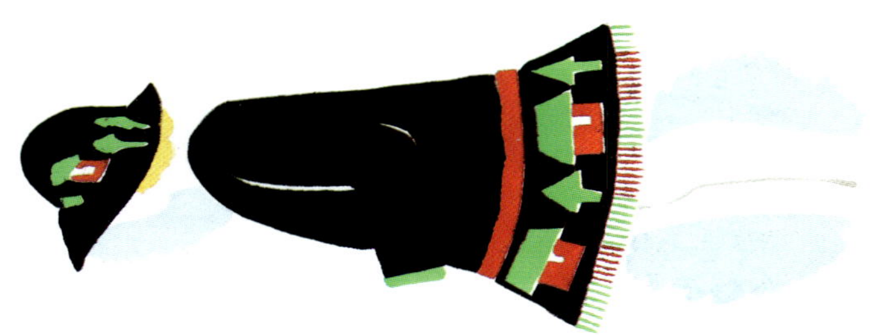

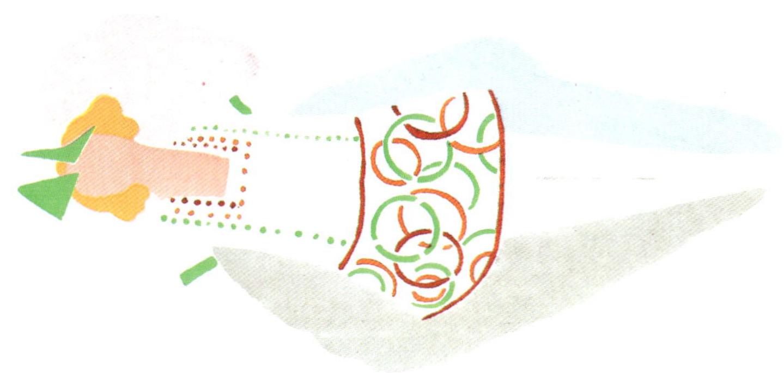

1920

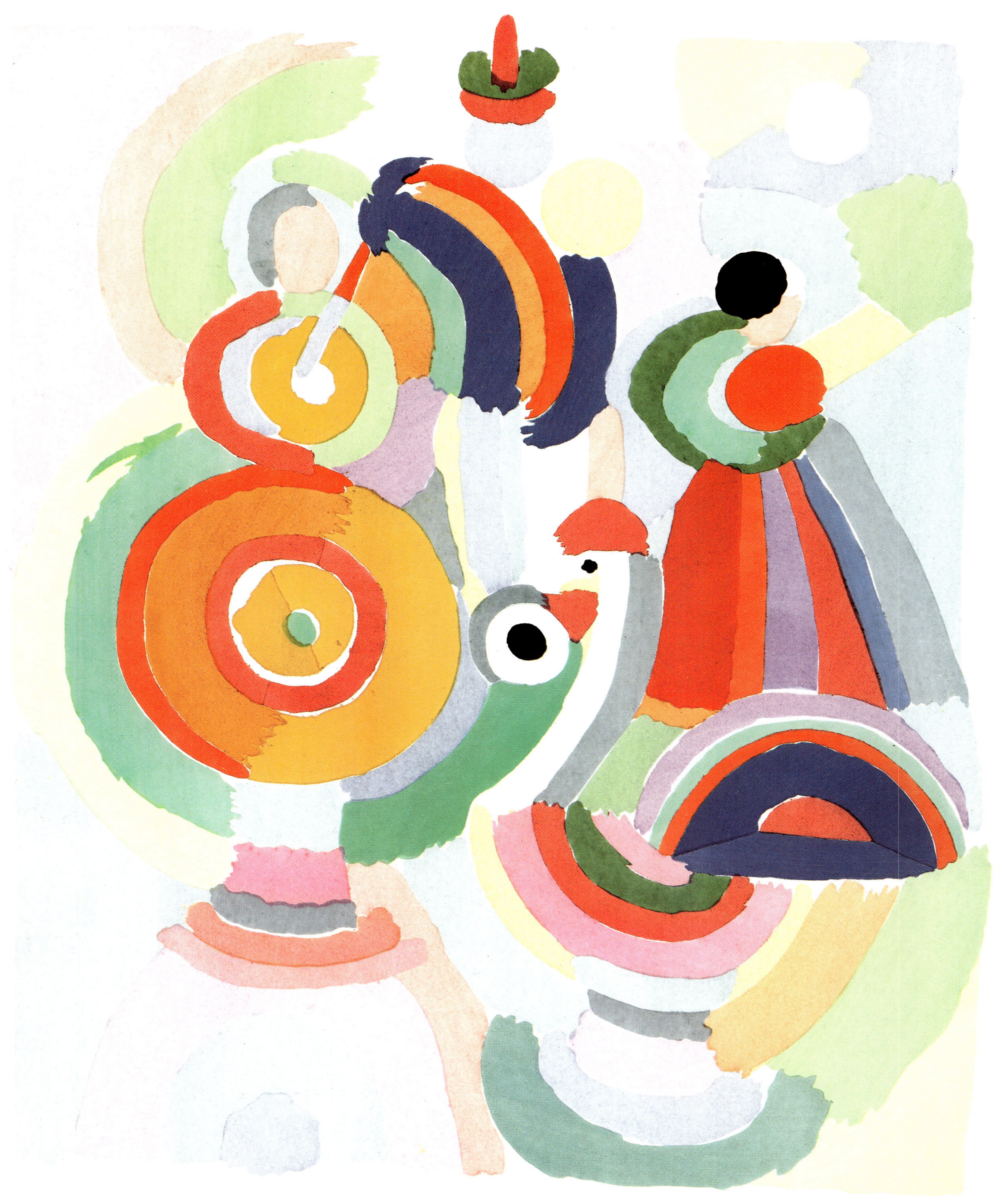

1915

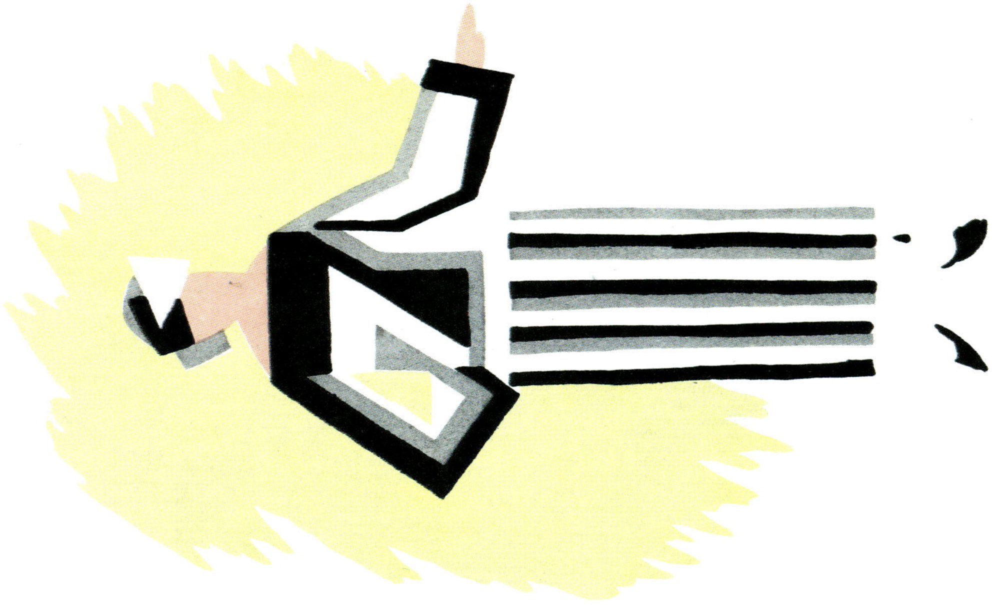

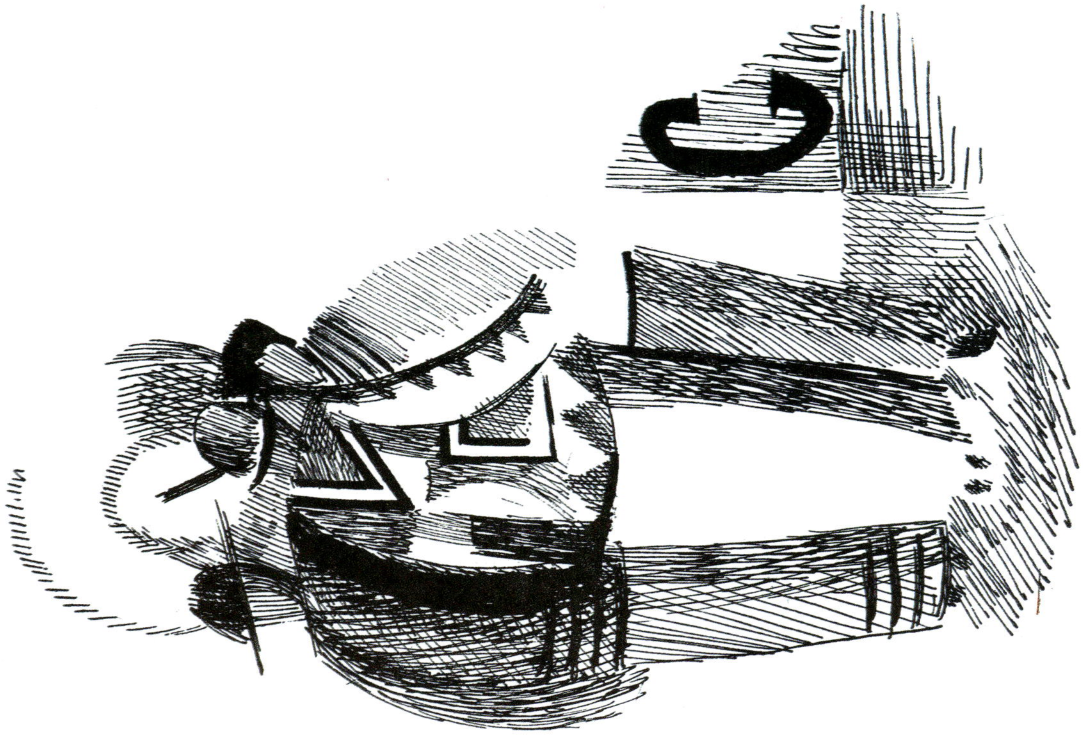

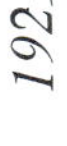

1923

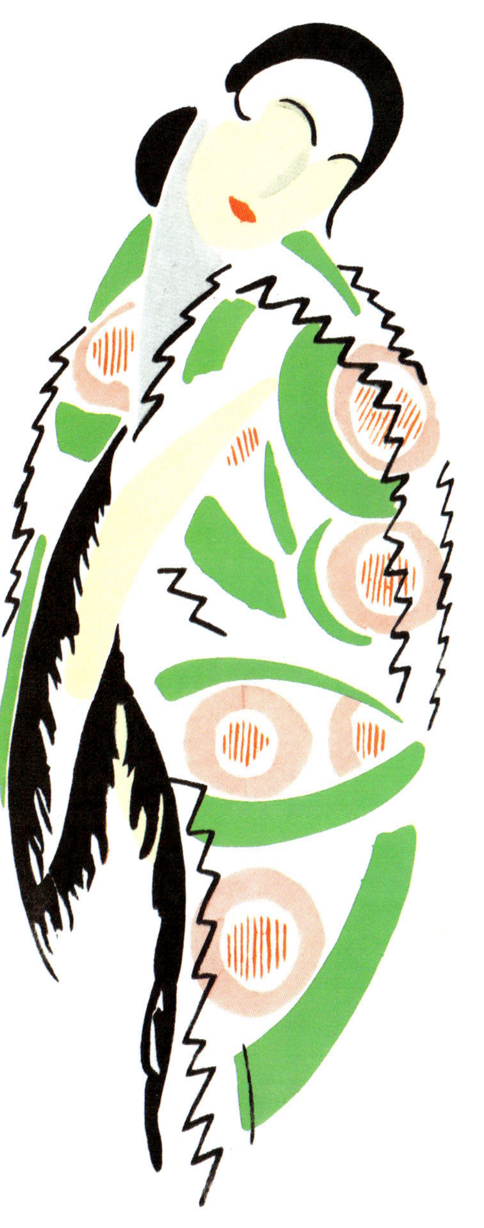

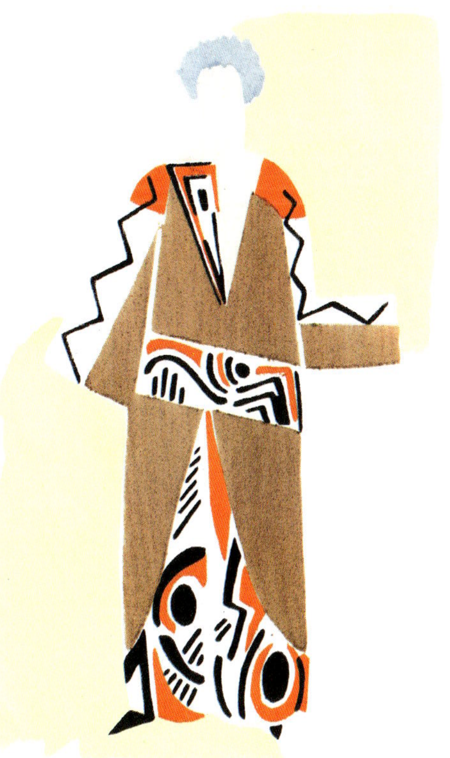

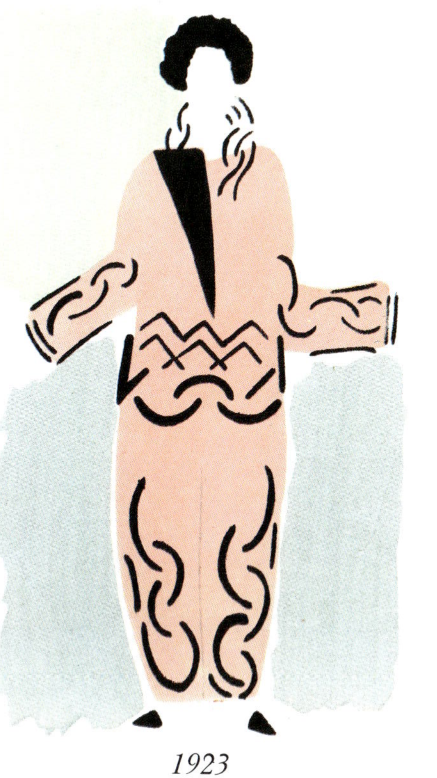

1923

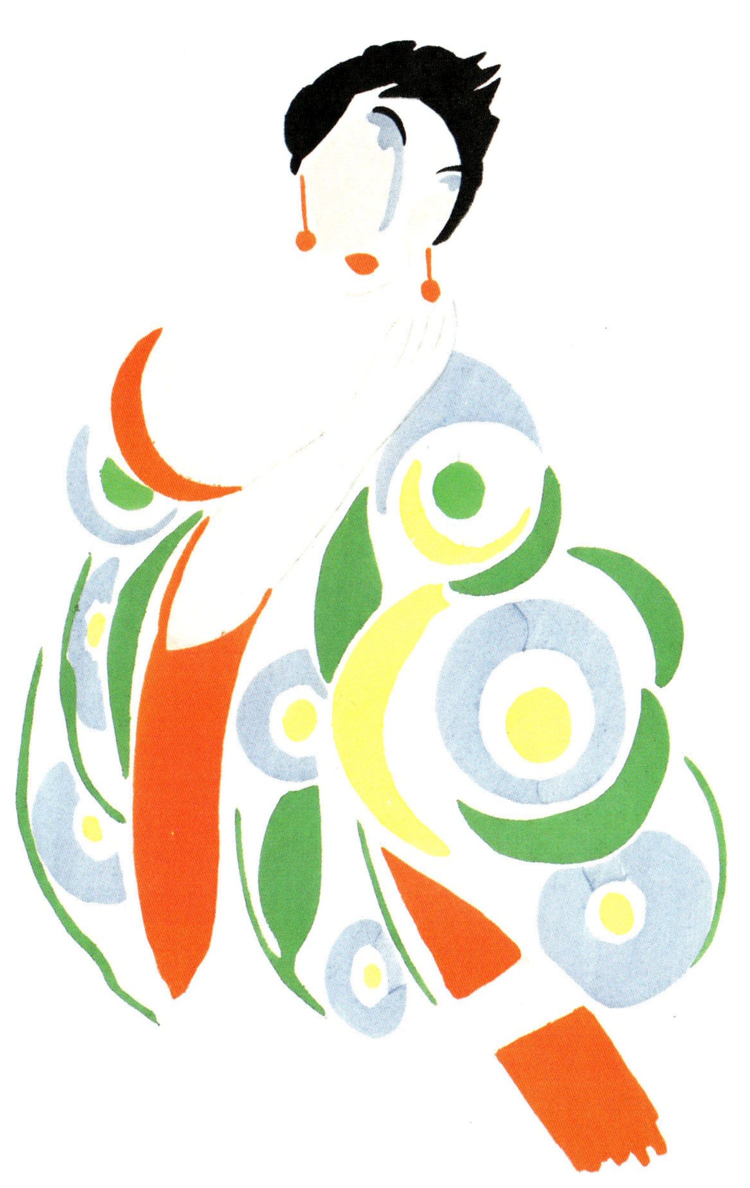

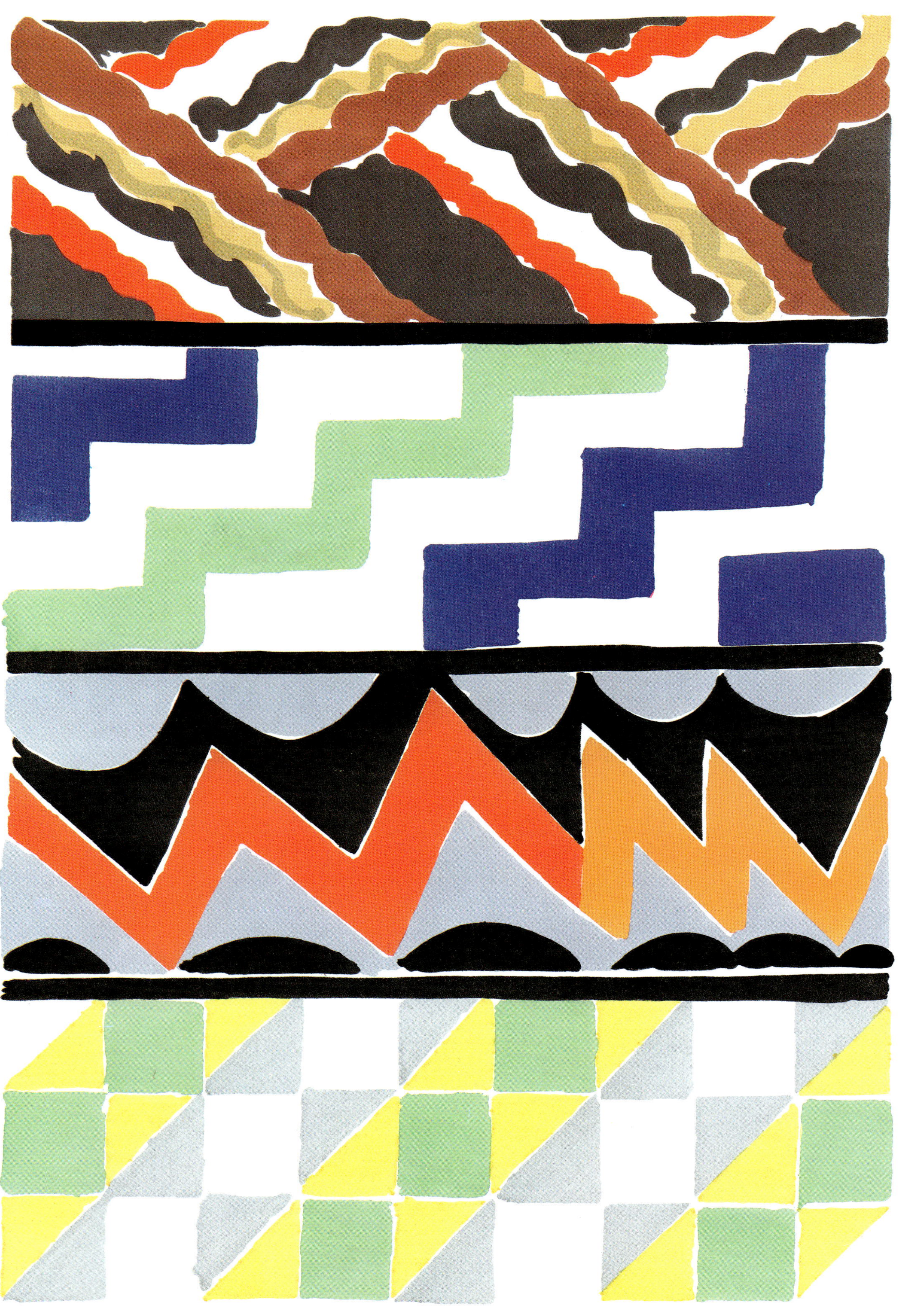

1924

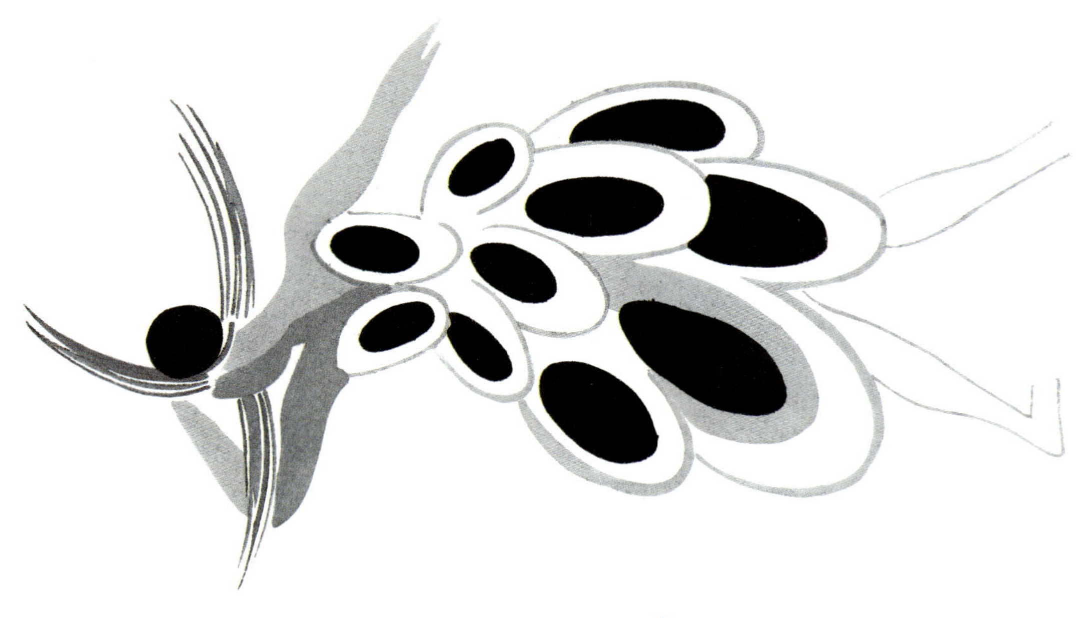

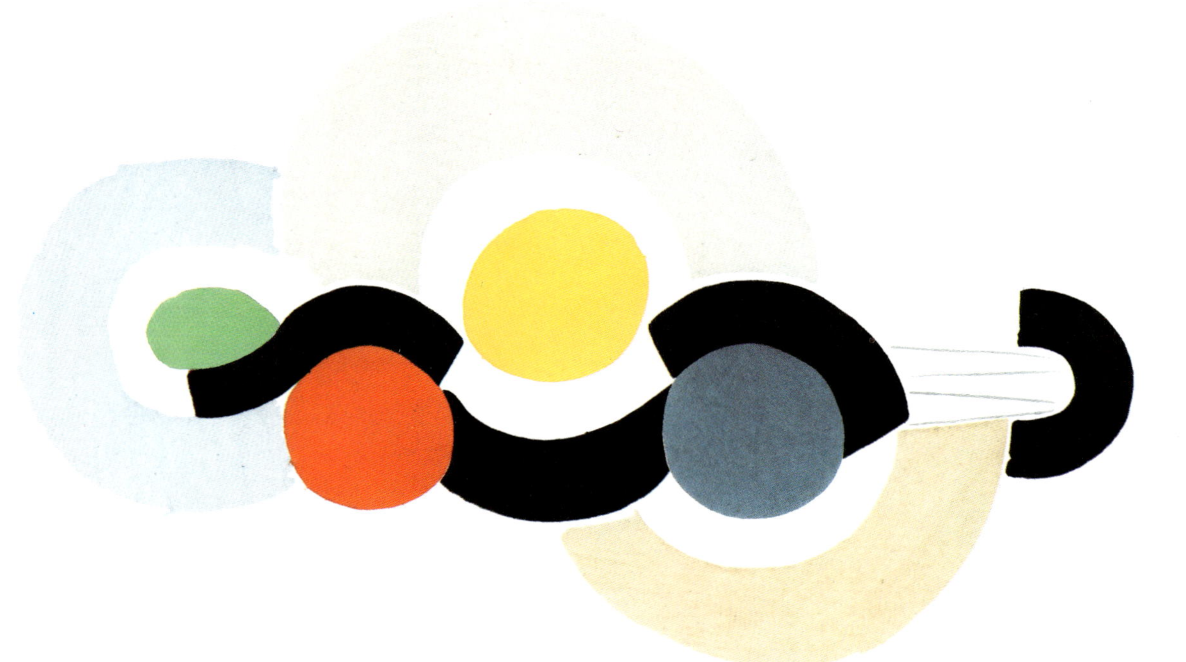

1919–1923

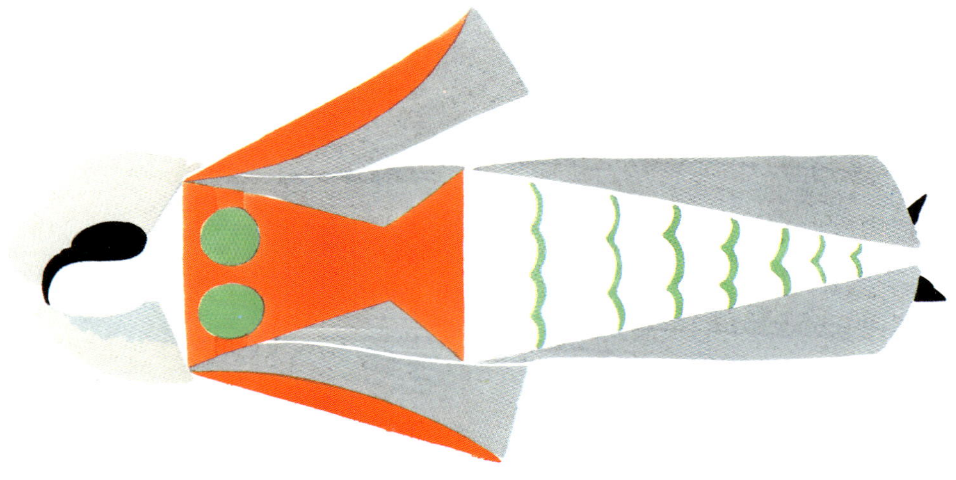

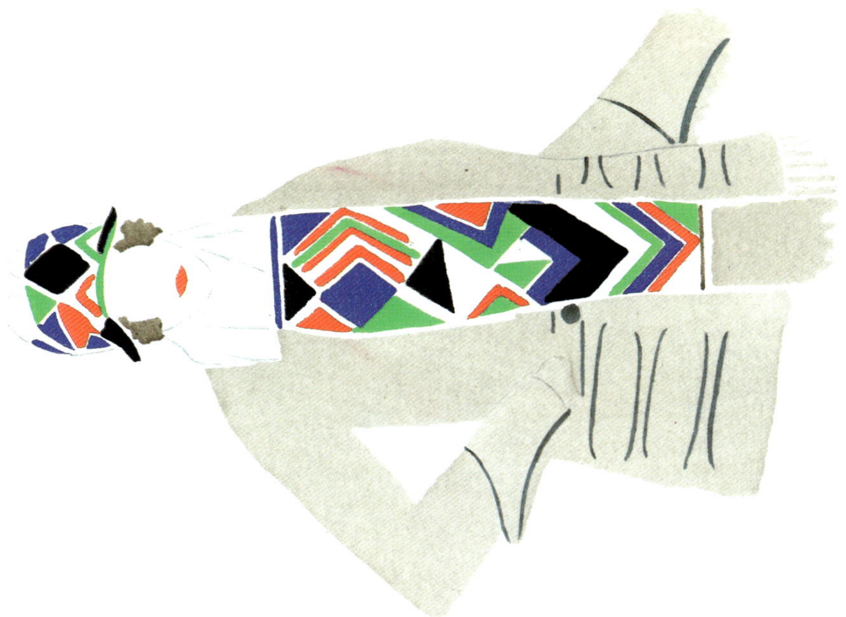

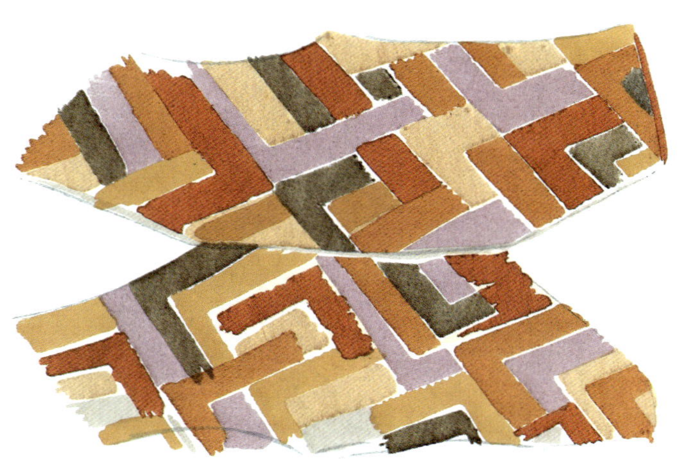

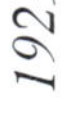

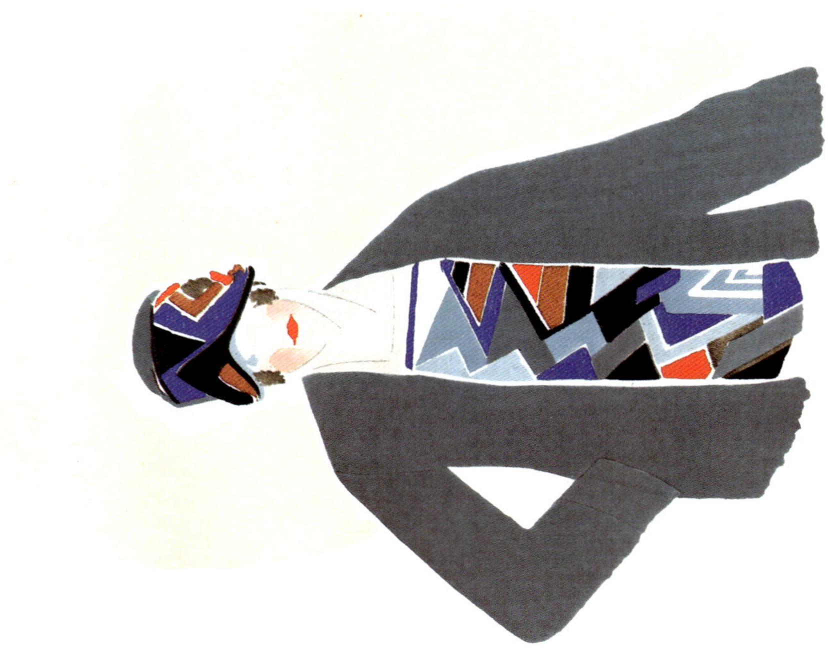

1923

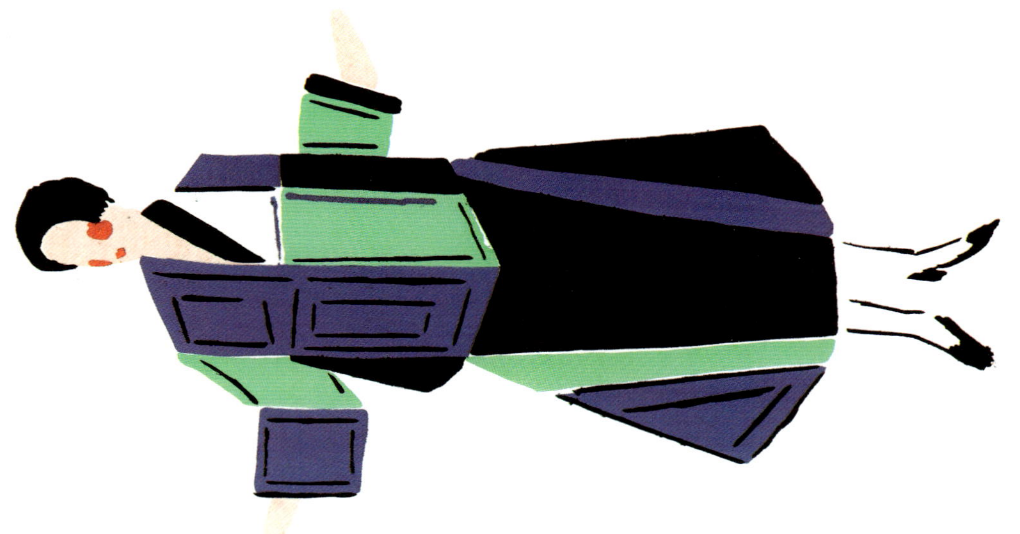

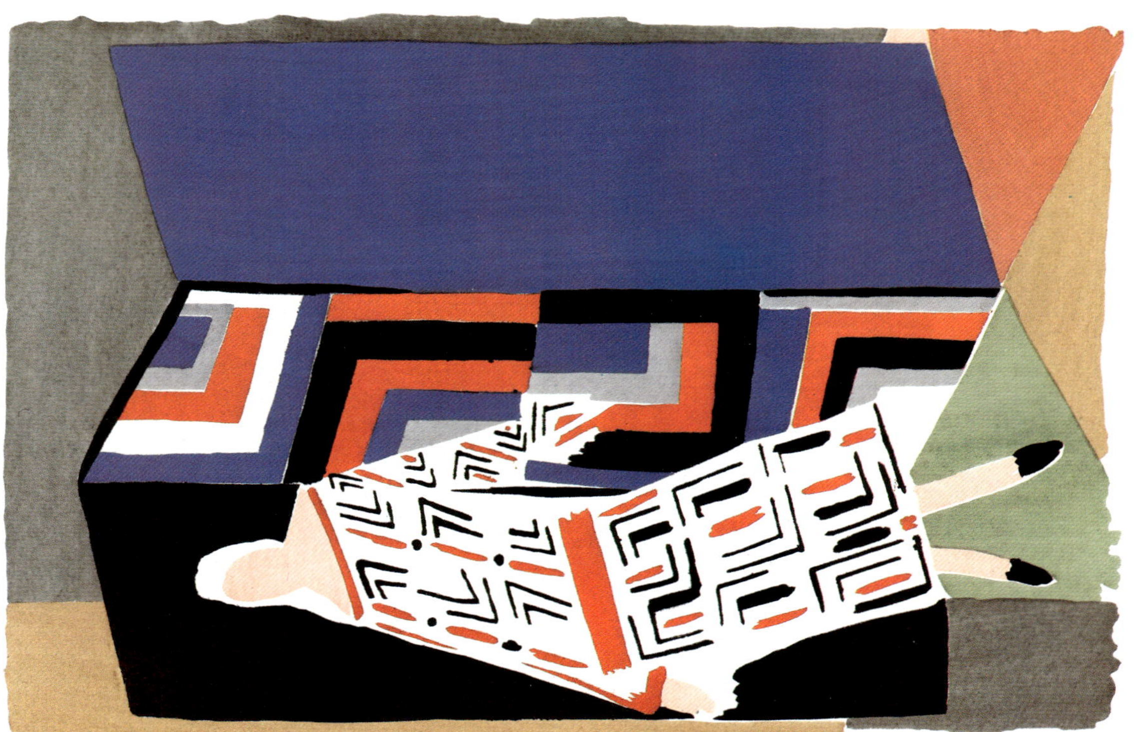

1924–1925

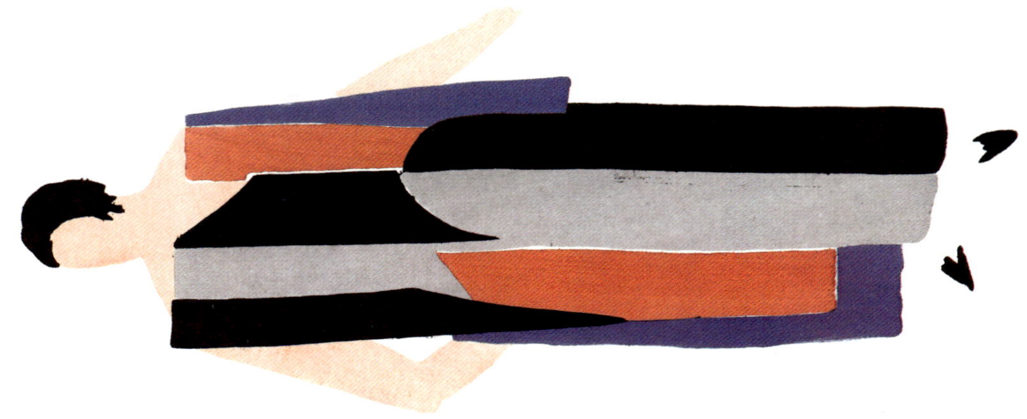

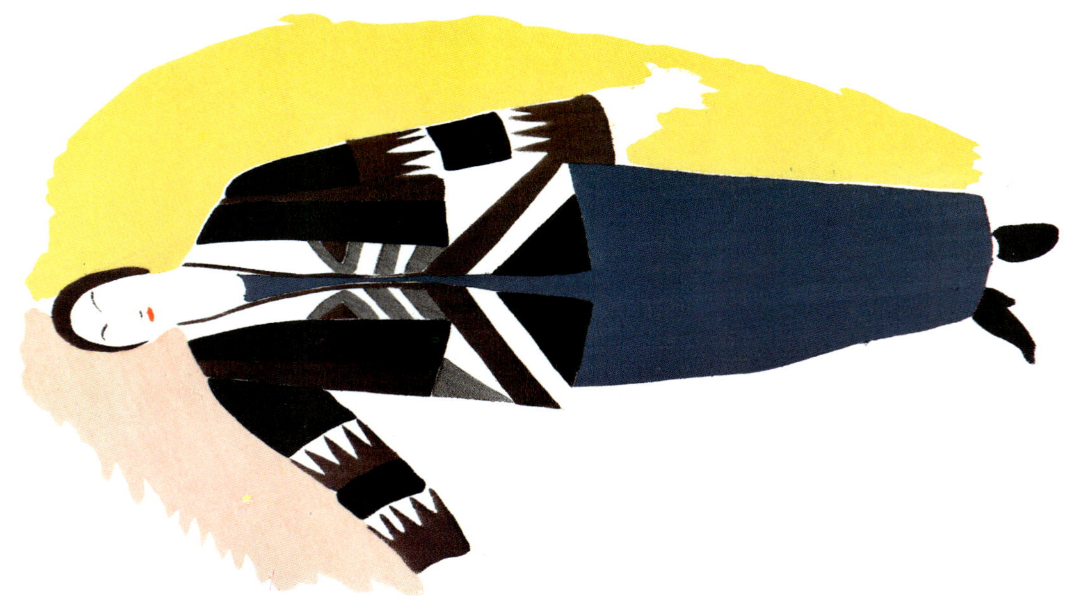

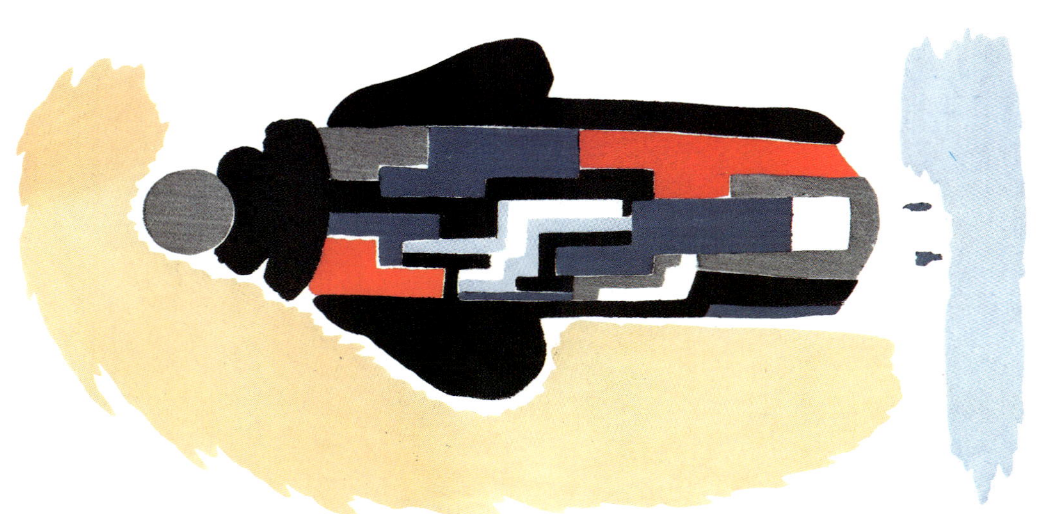

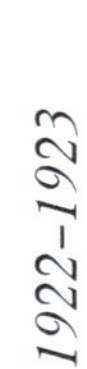

1922–1923

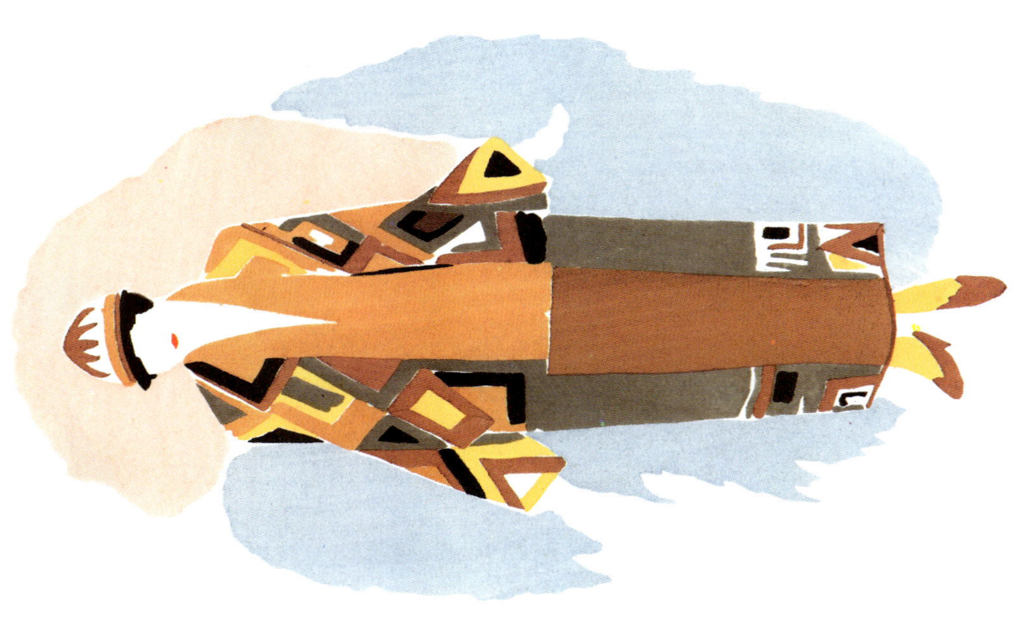

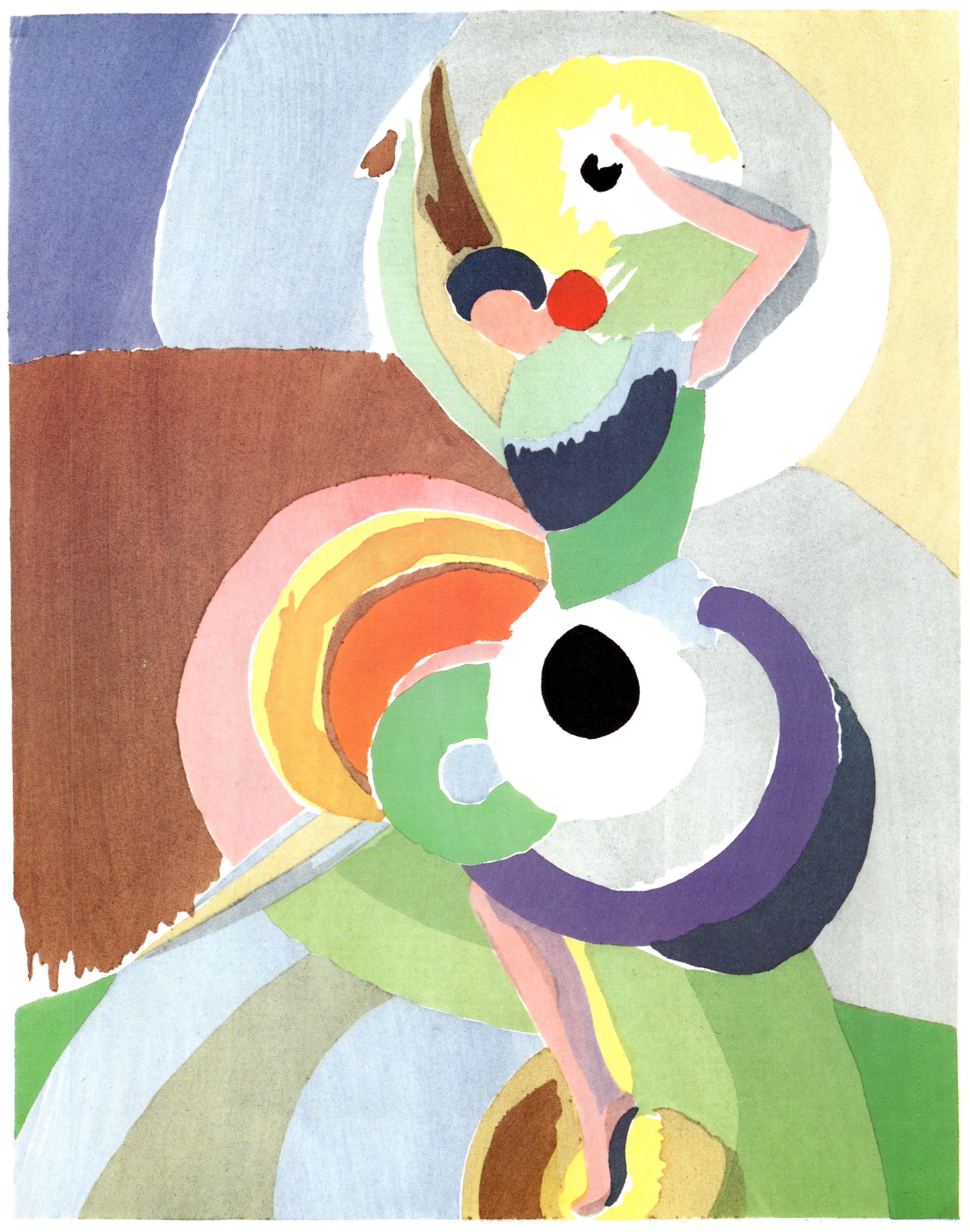

1924

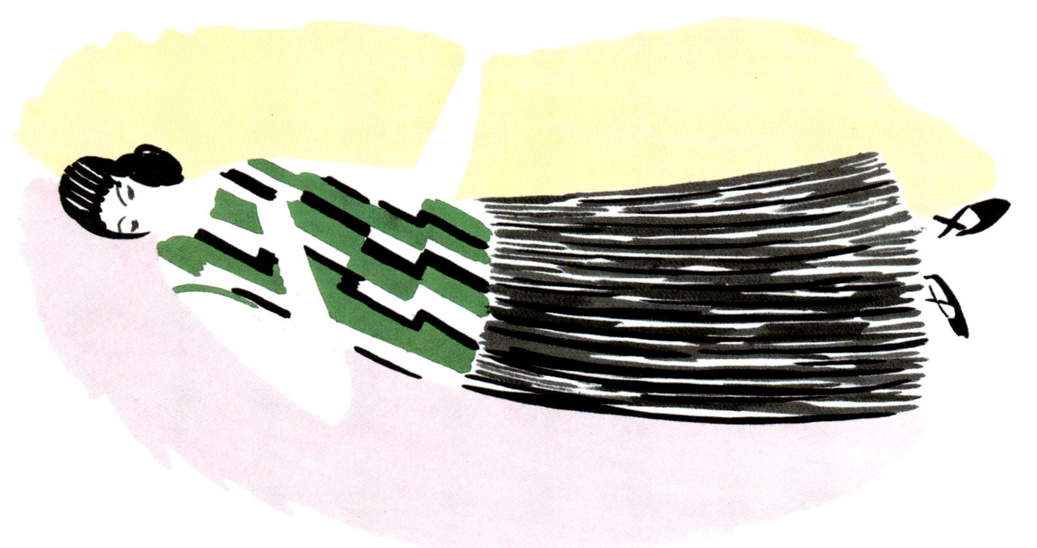

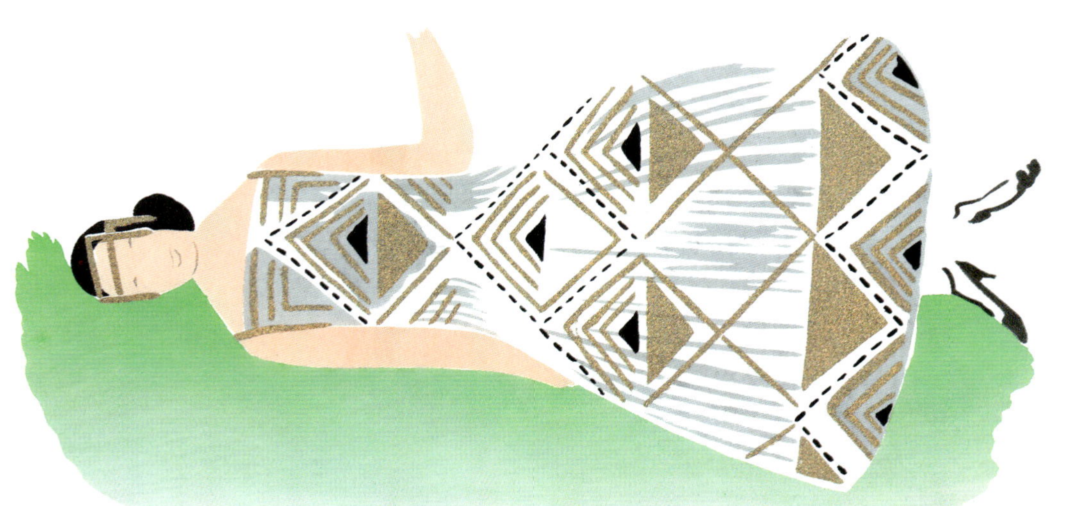

1923

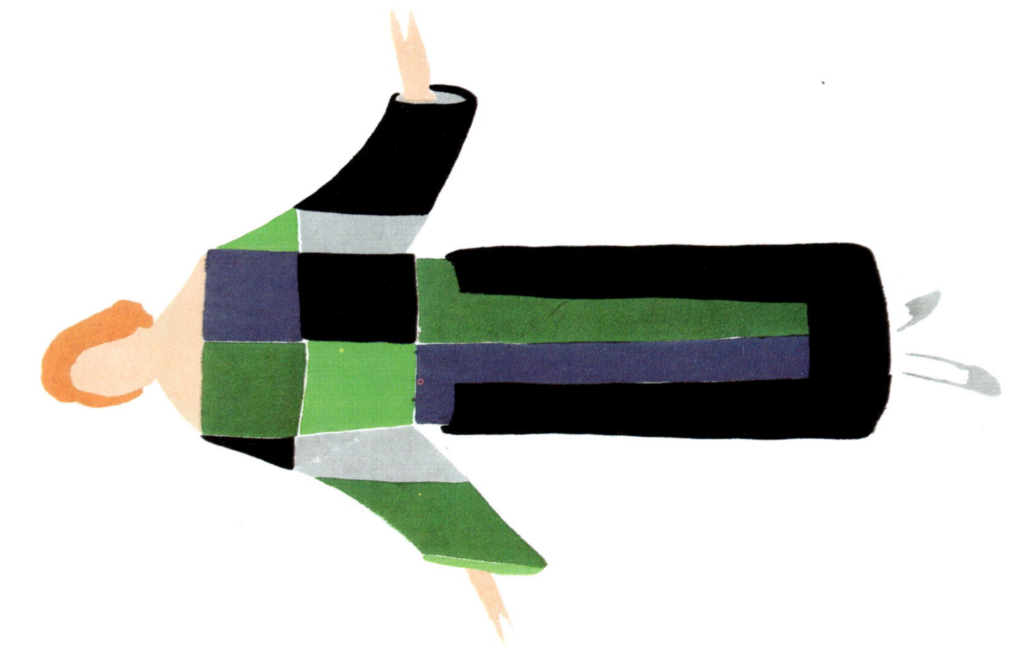

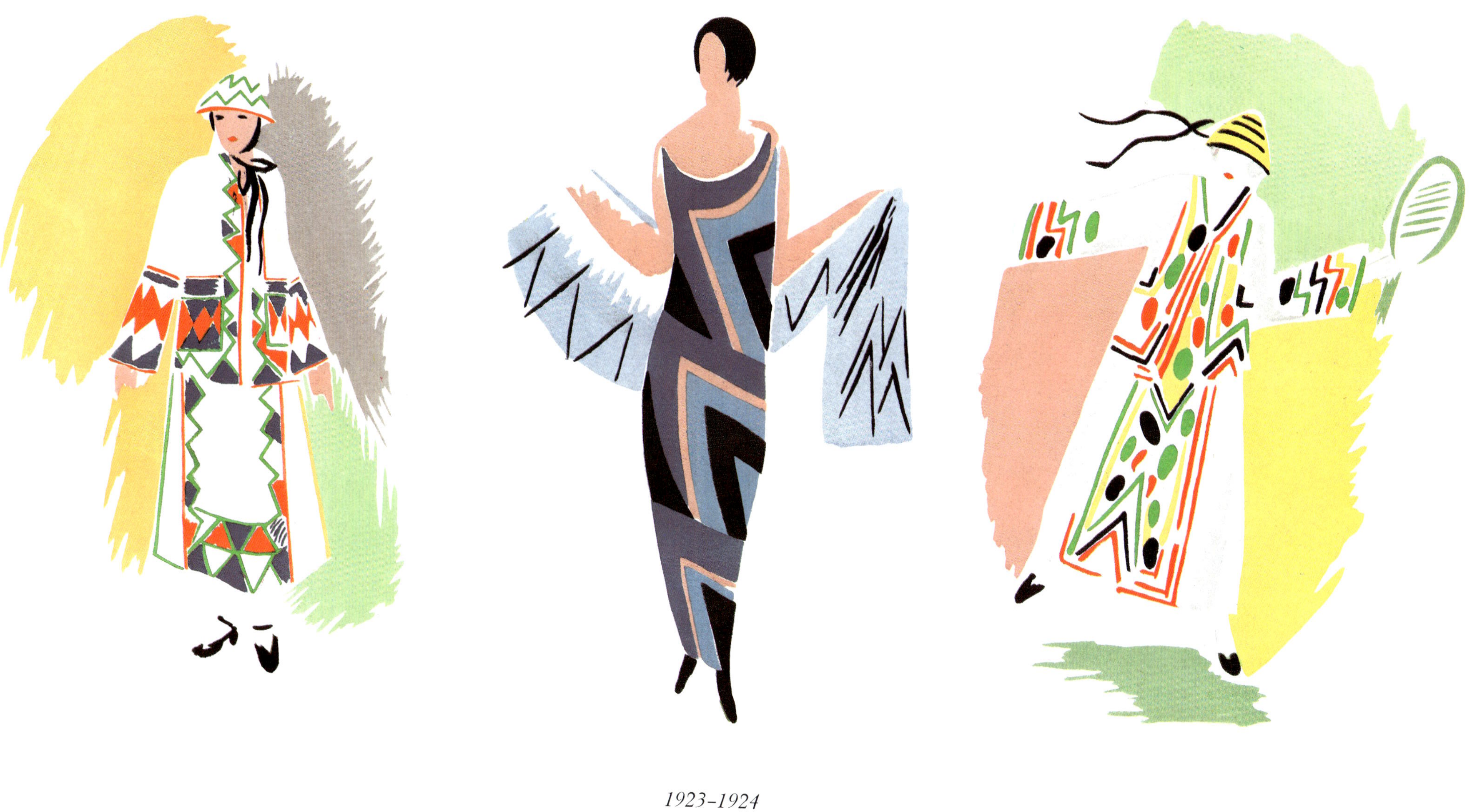

1923–1924

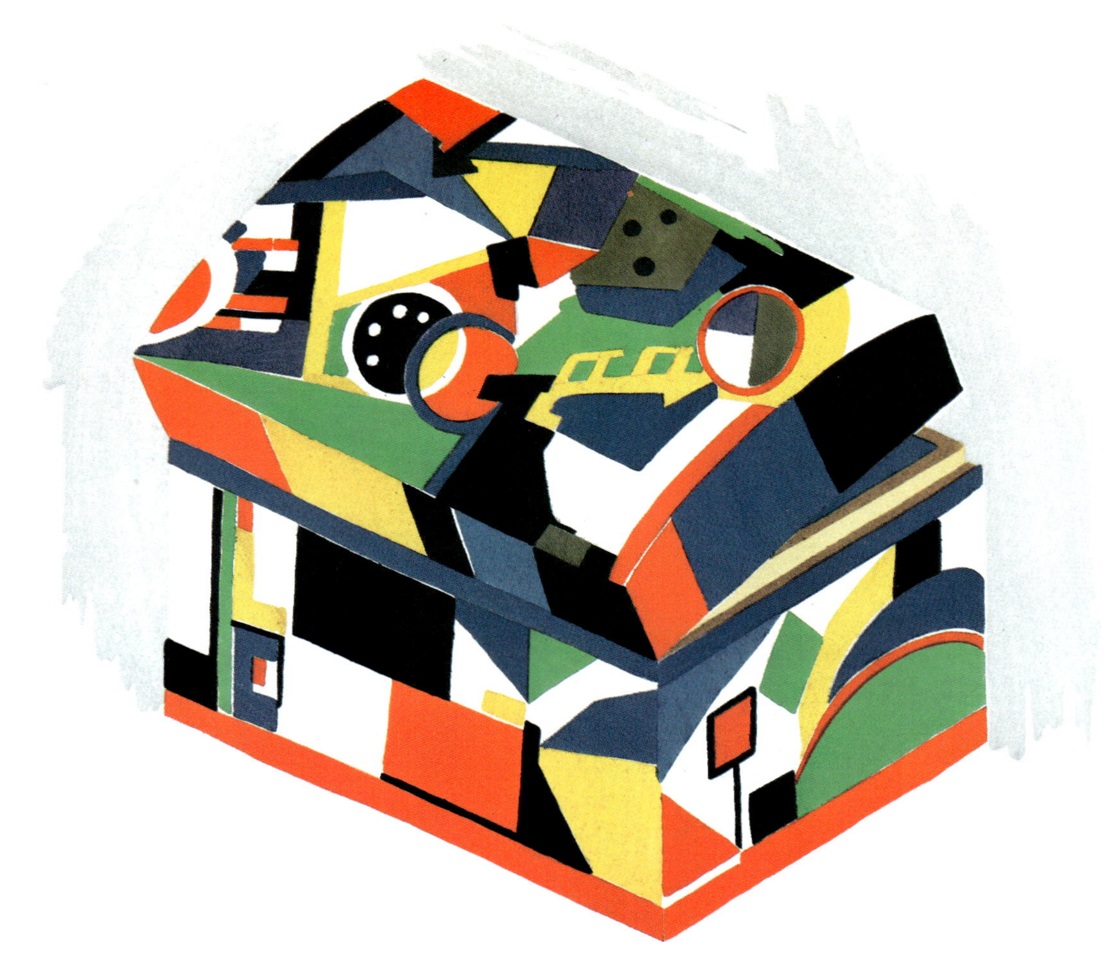

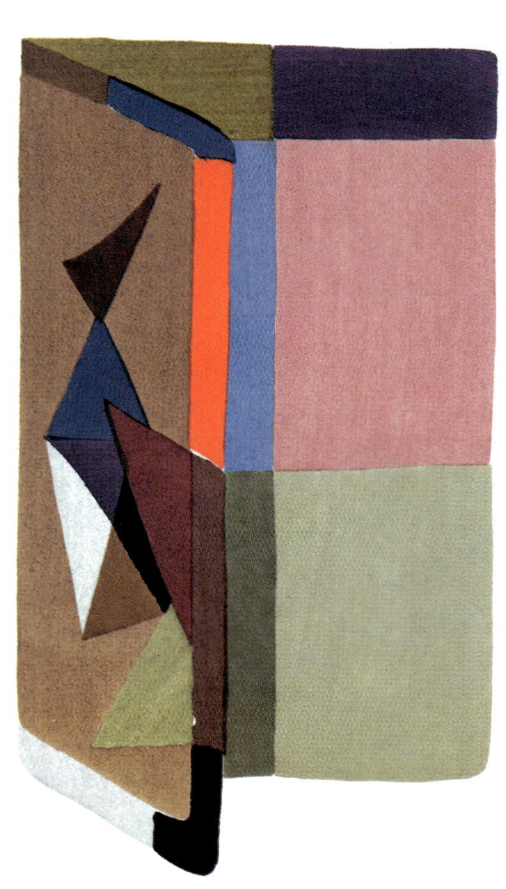

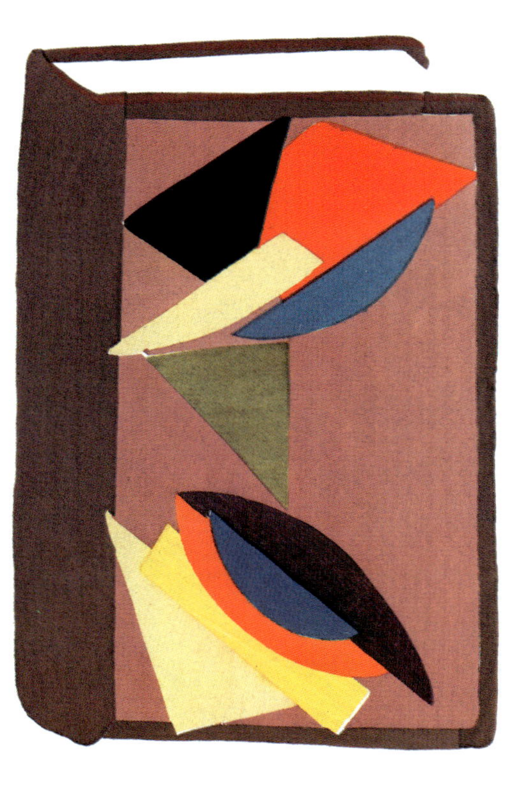

1912–1913

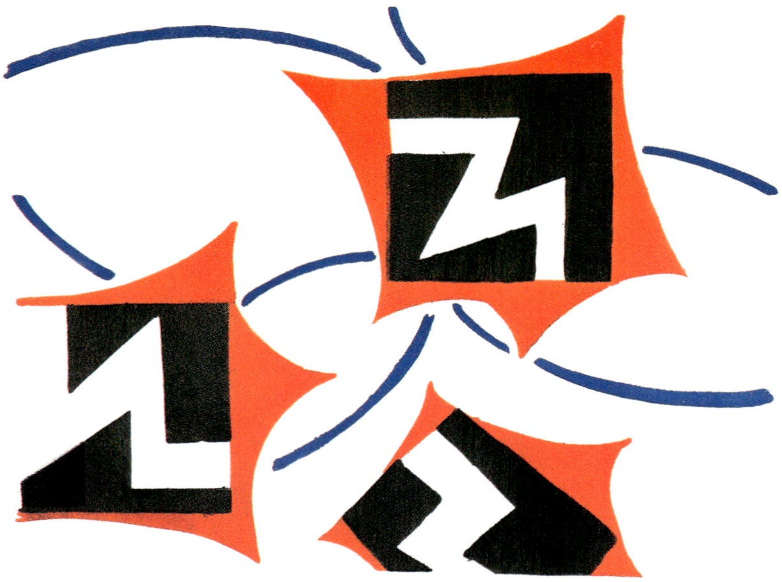

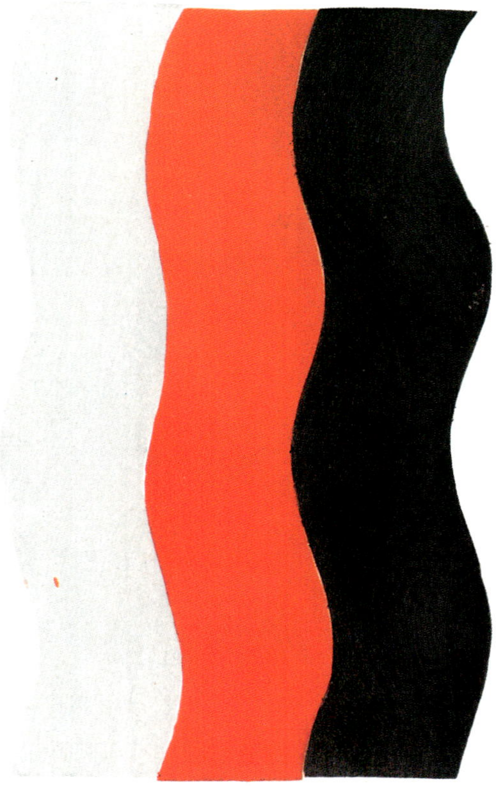

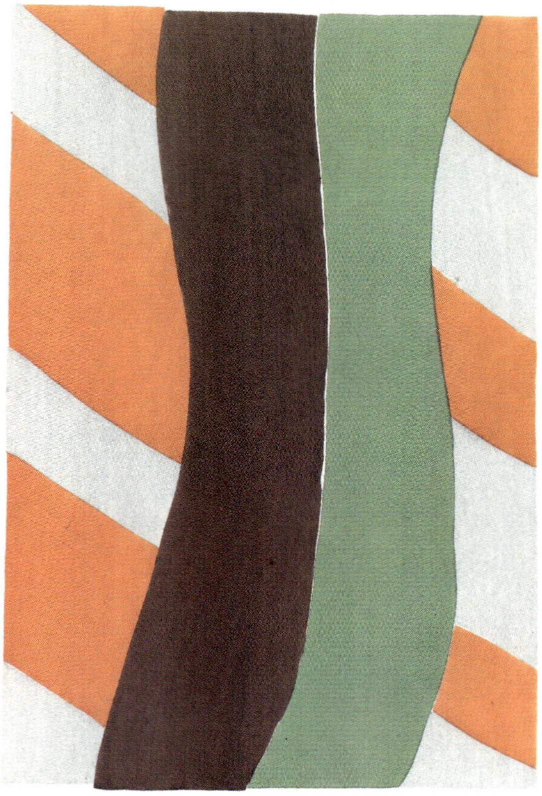

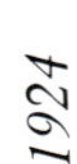

1924

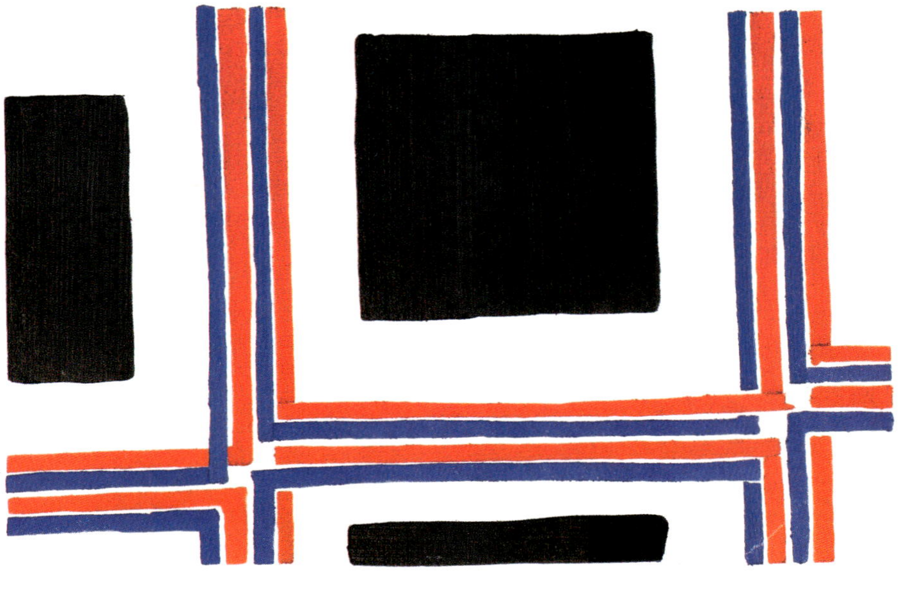

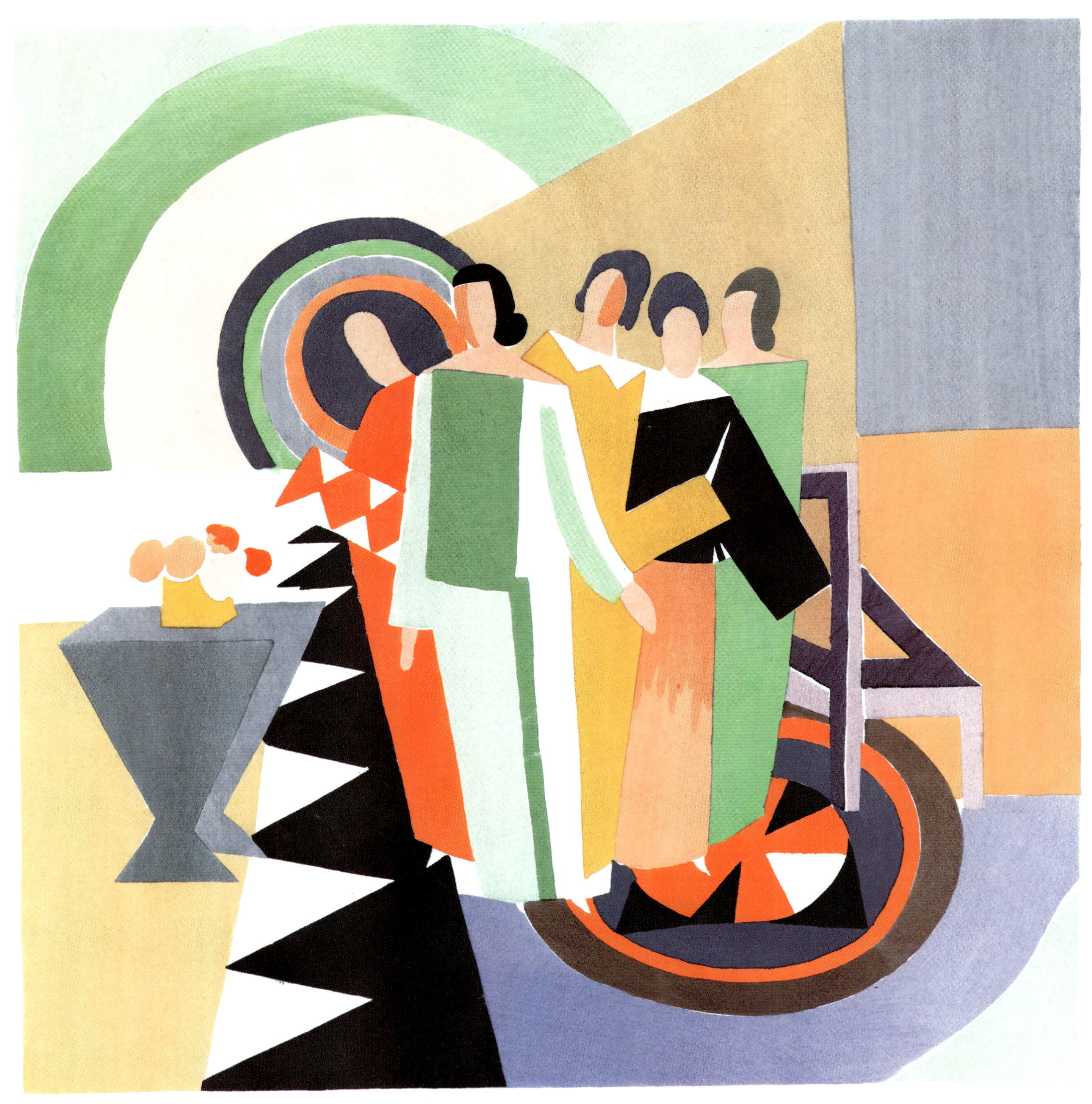

1924

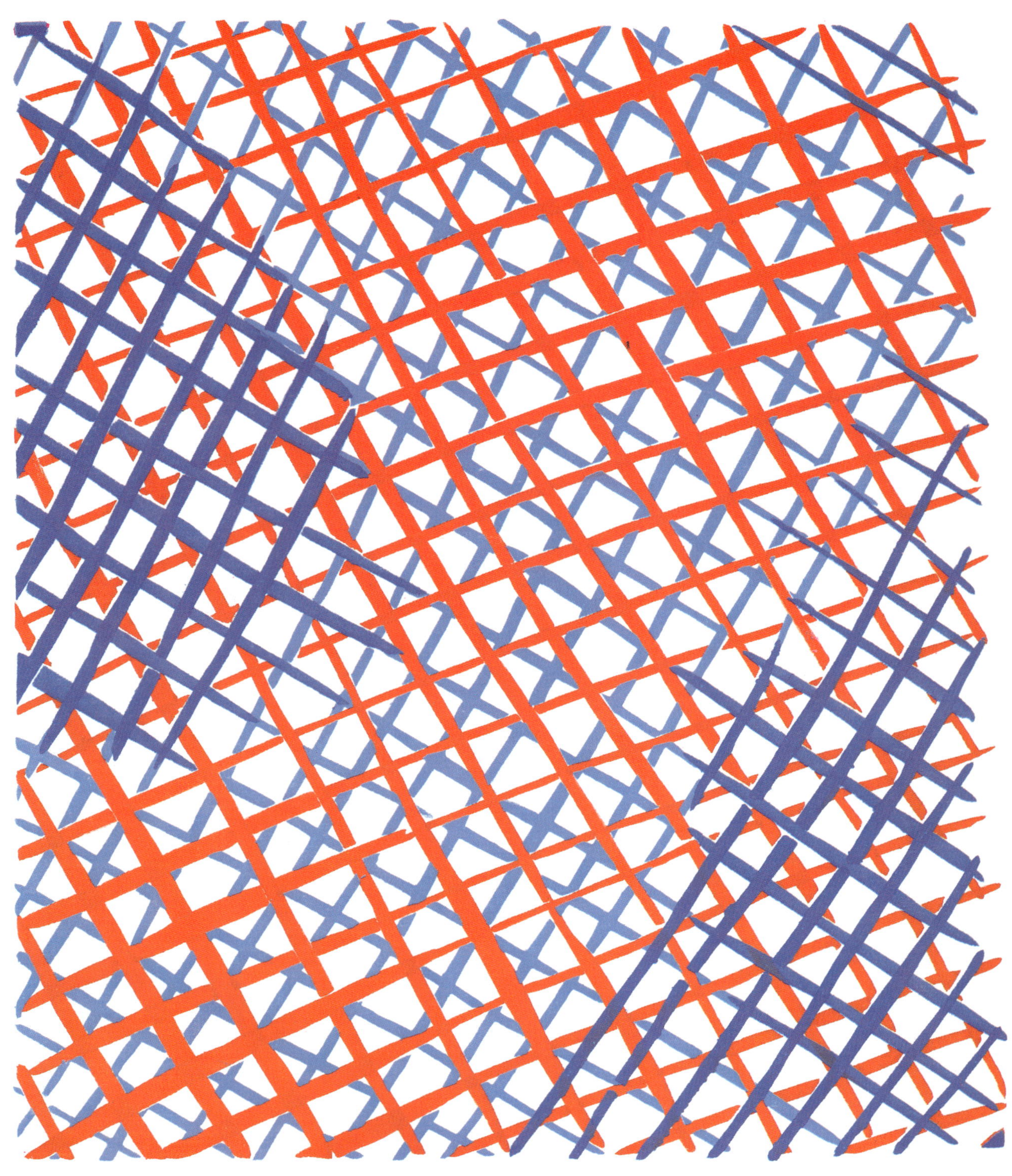

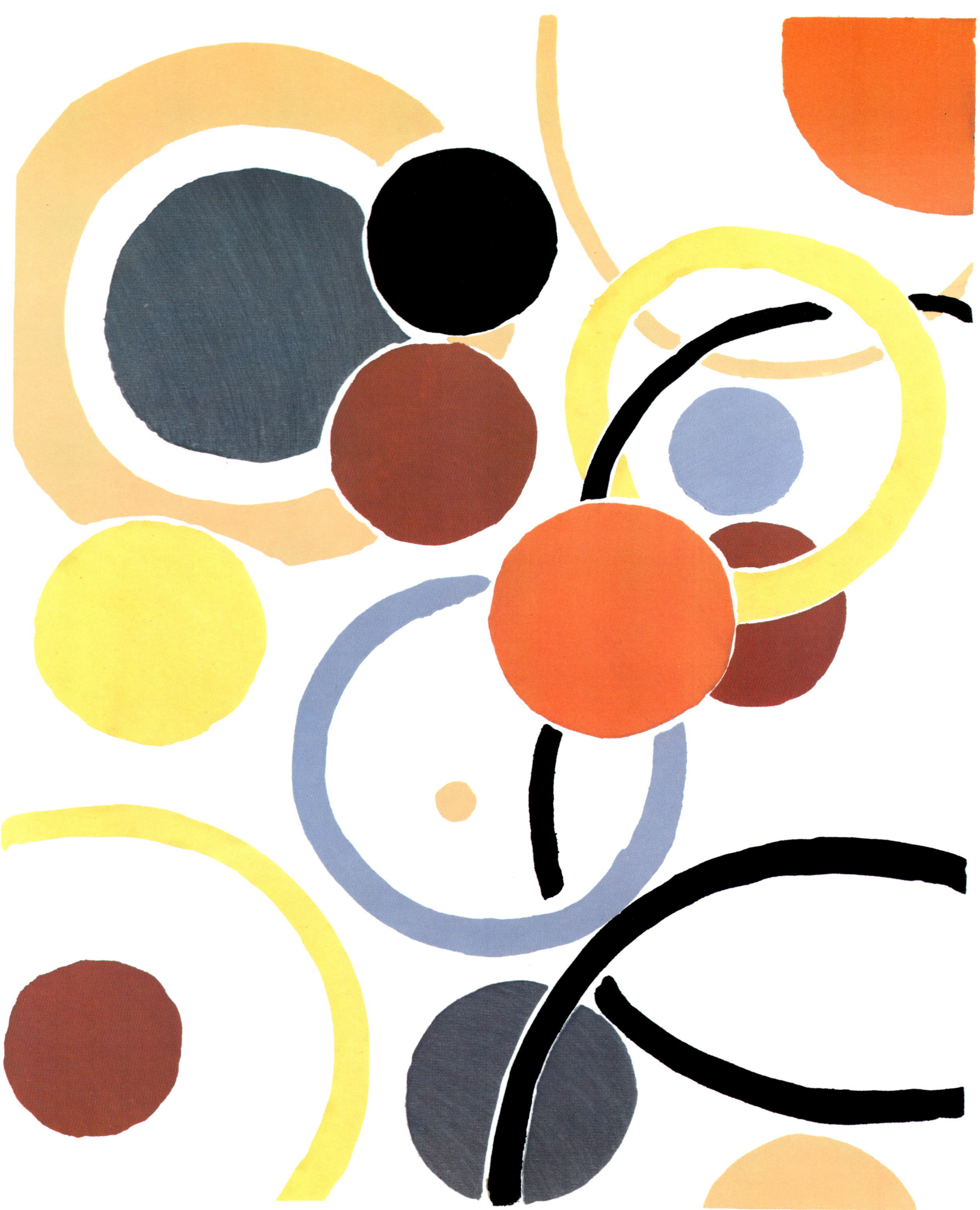

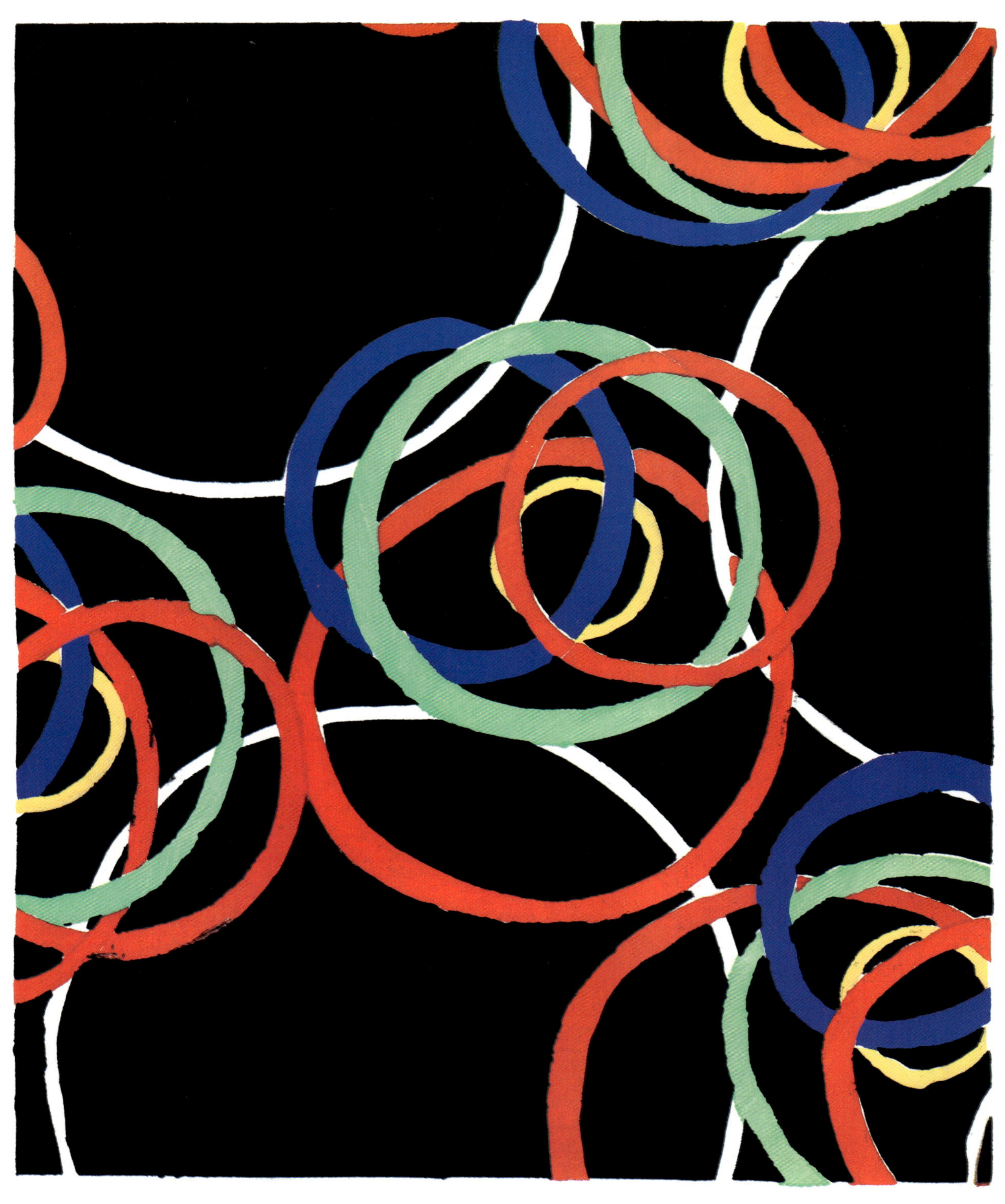

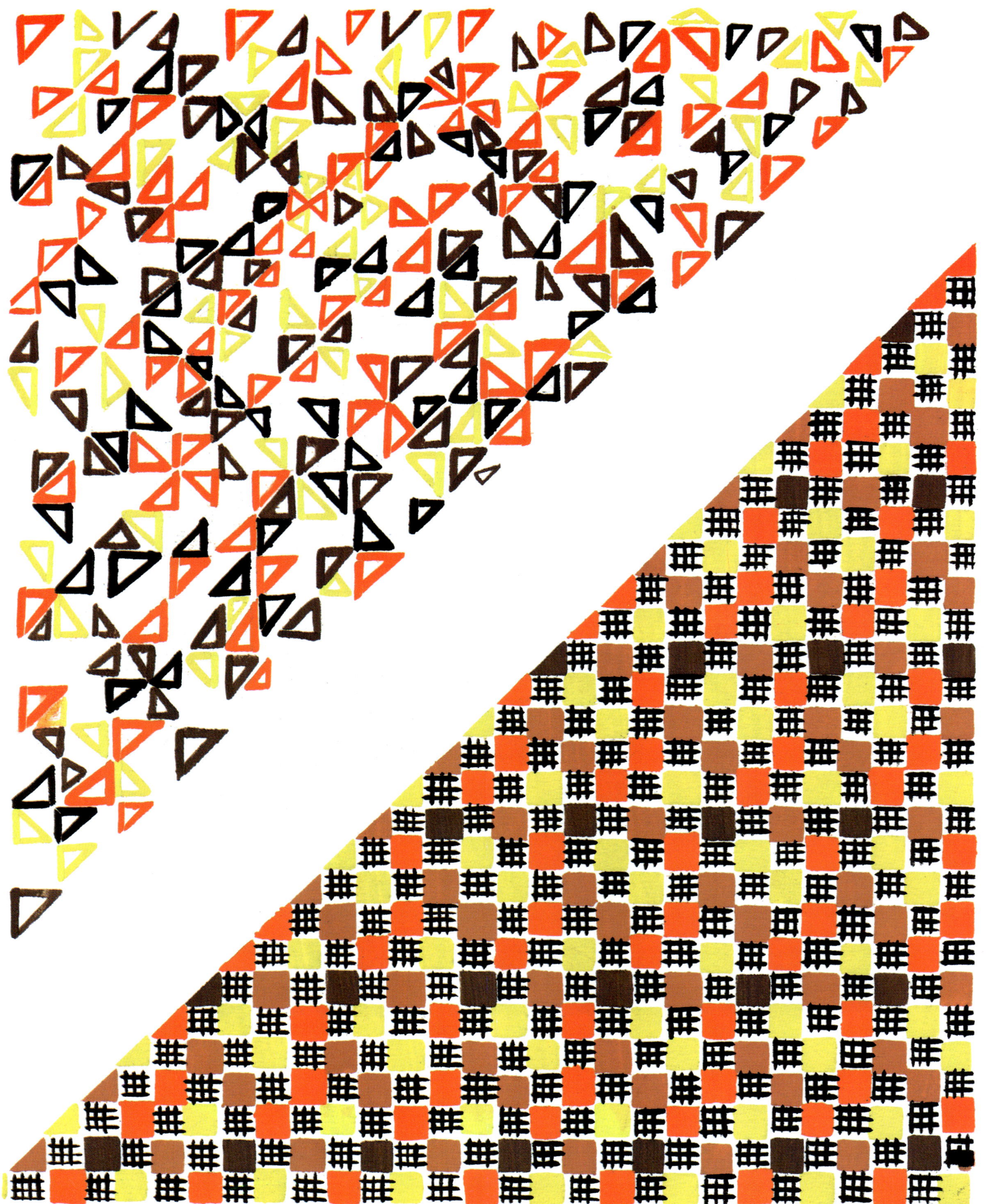

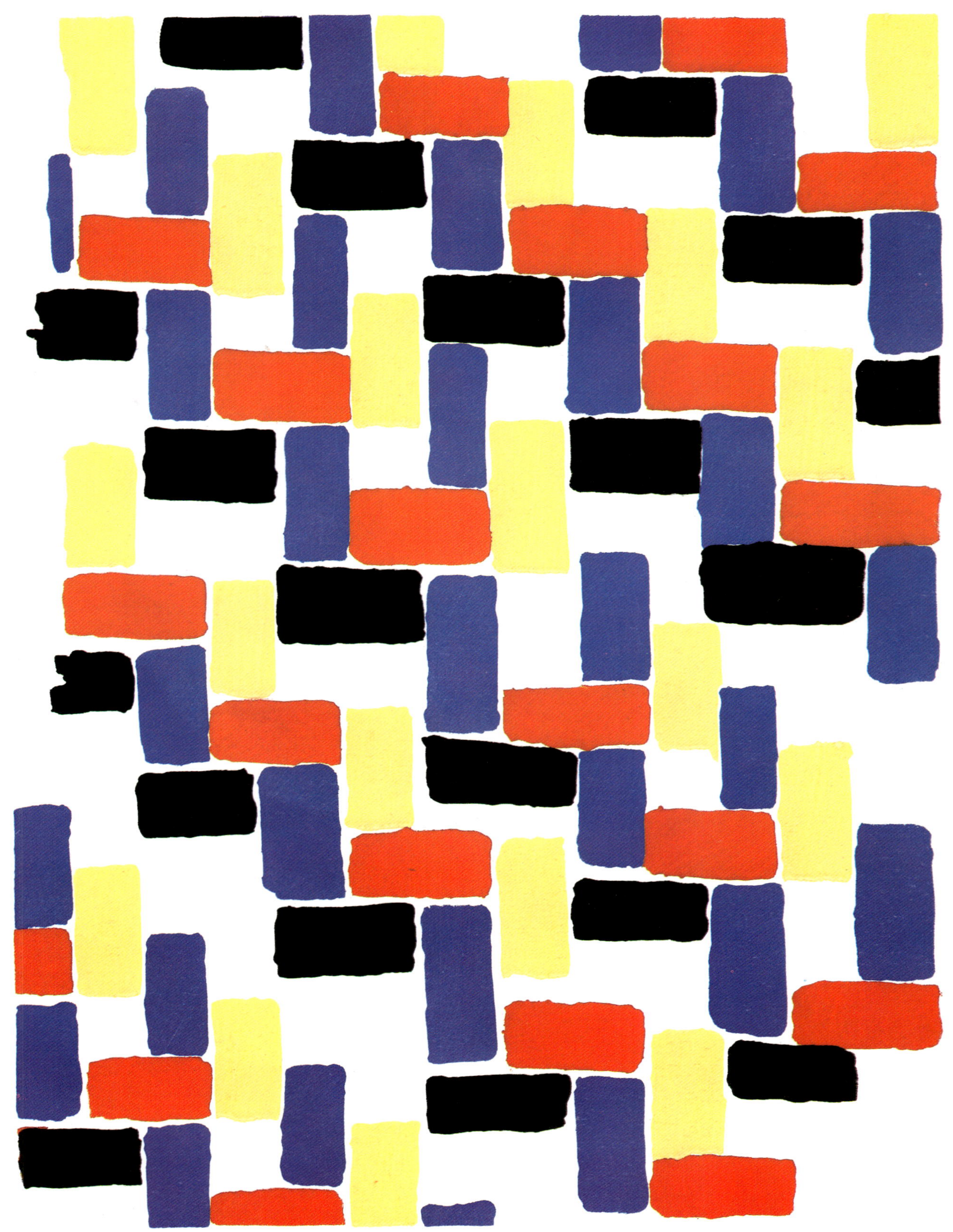

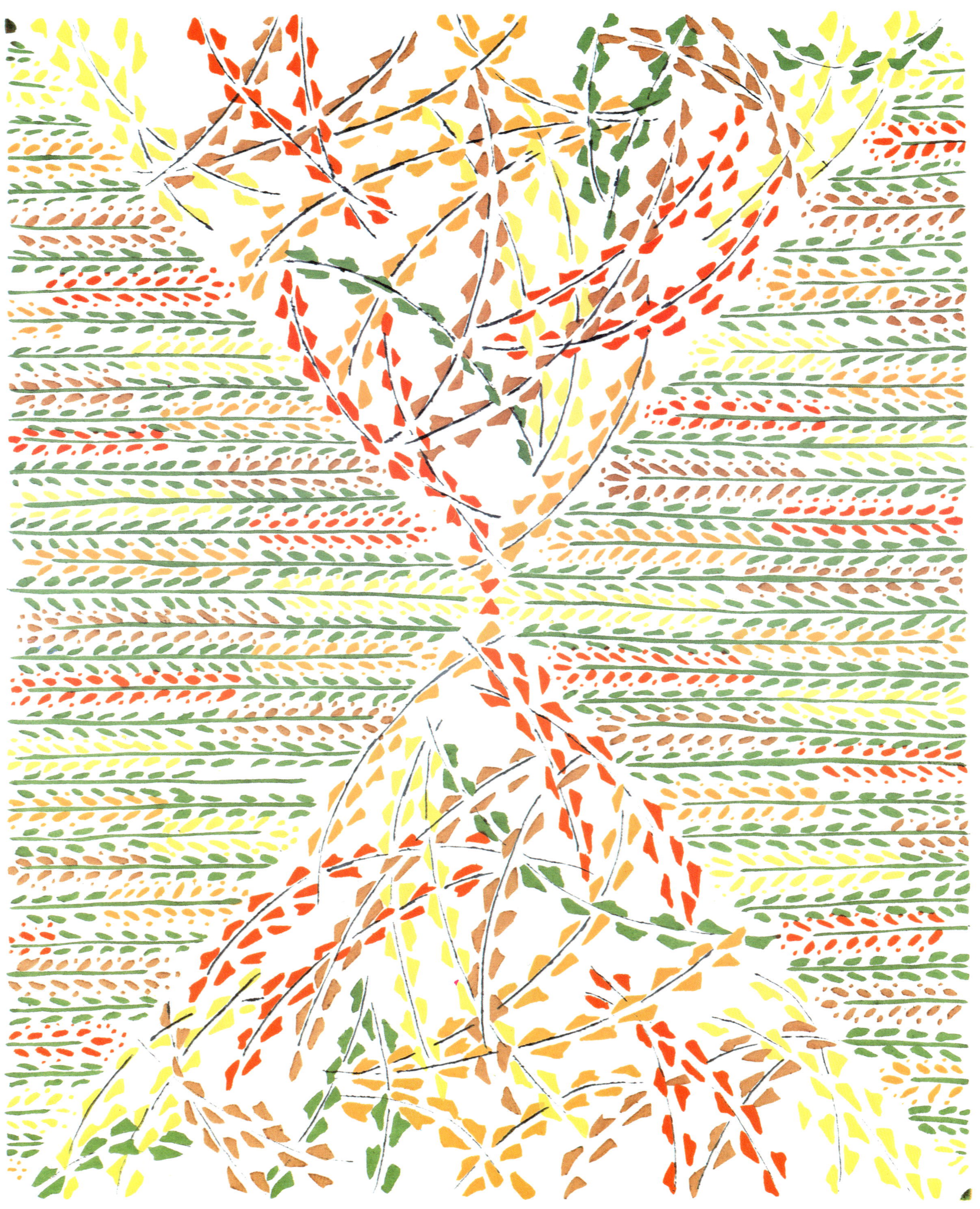

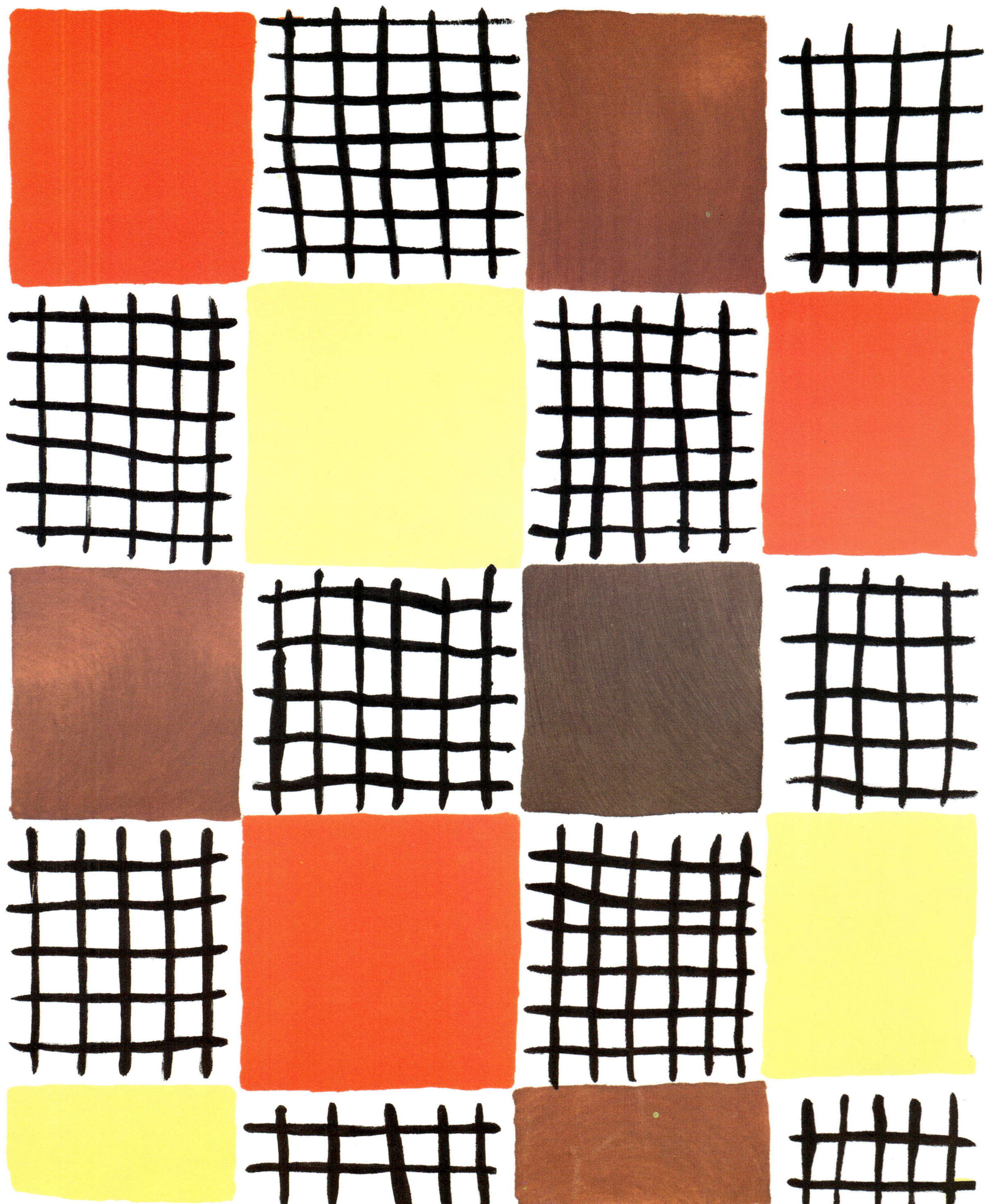

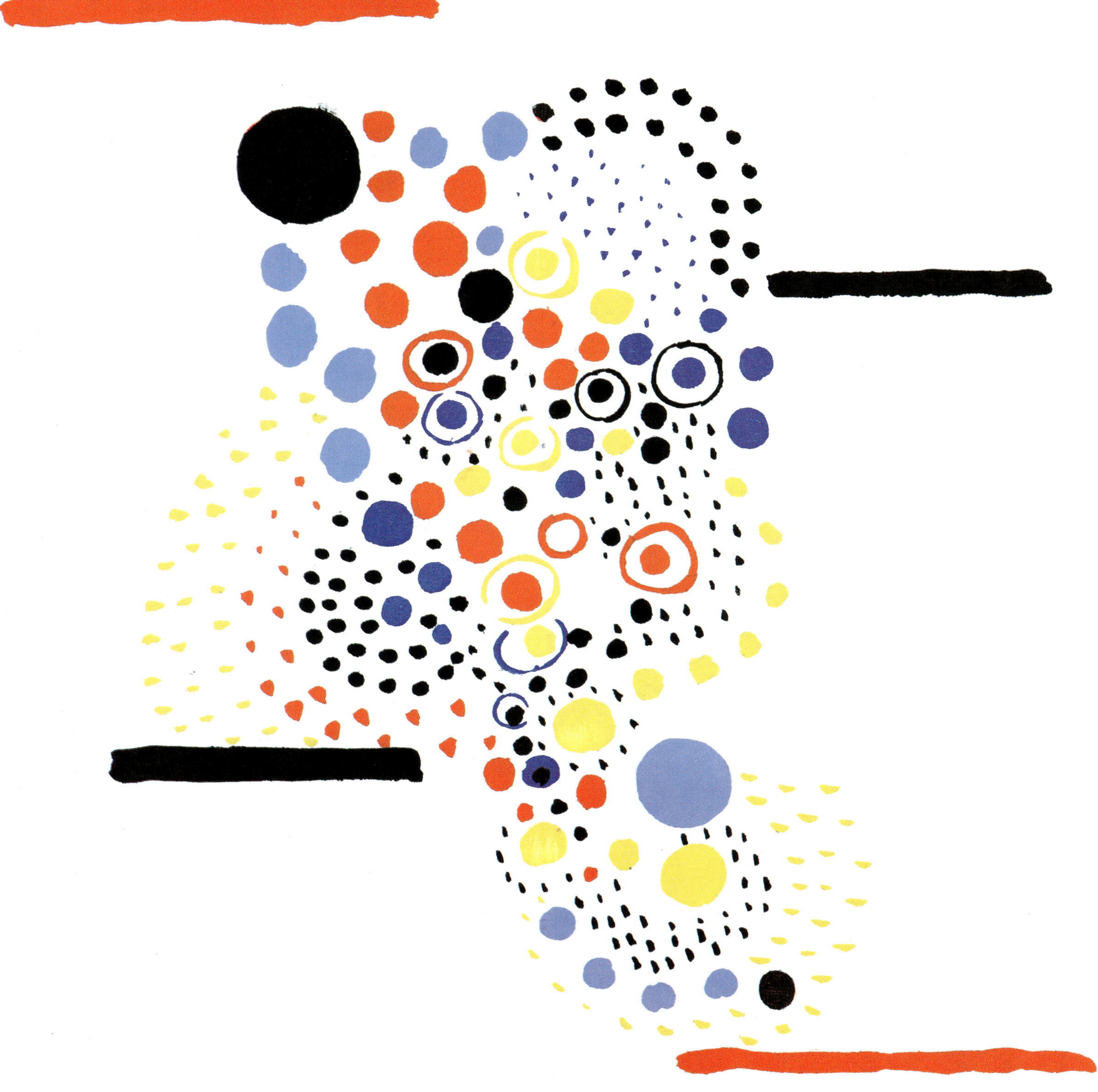

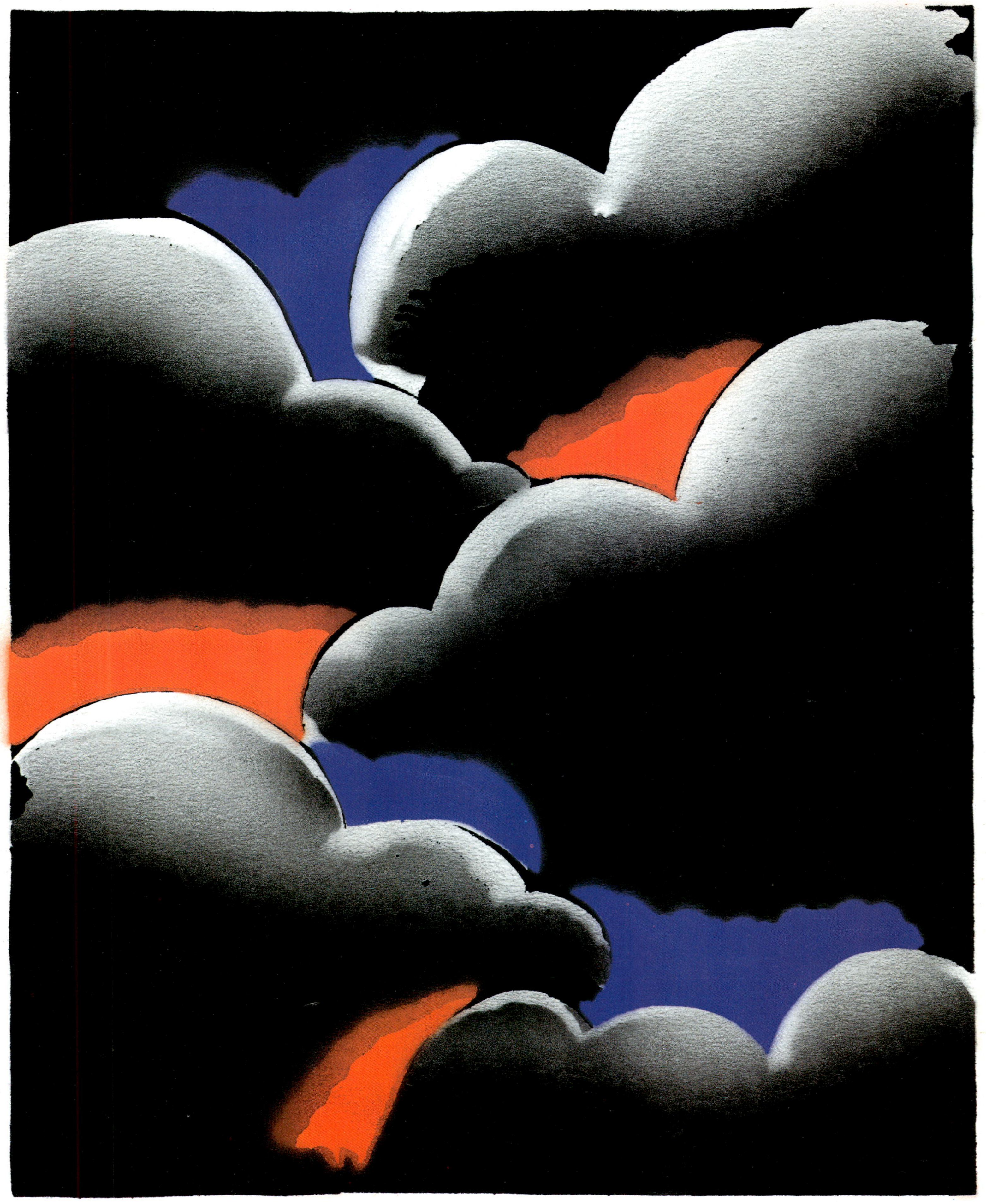

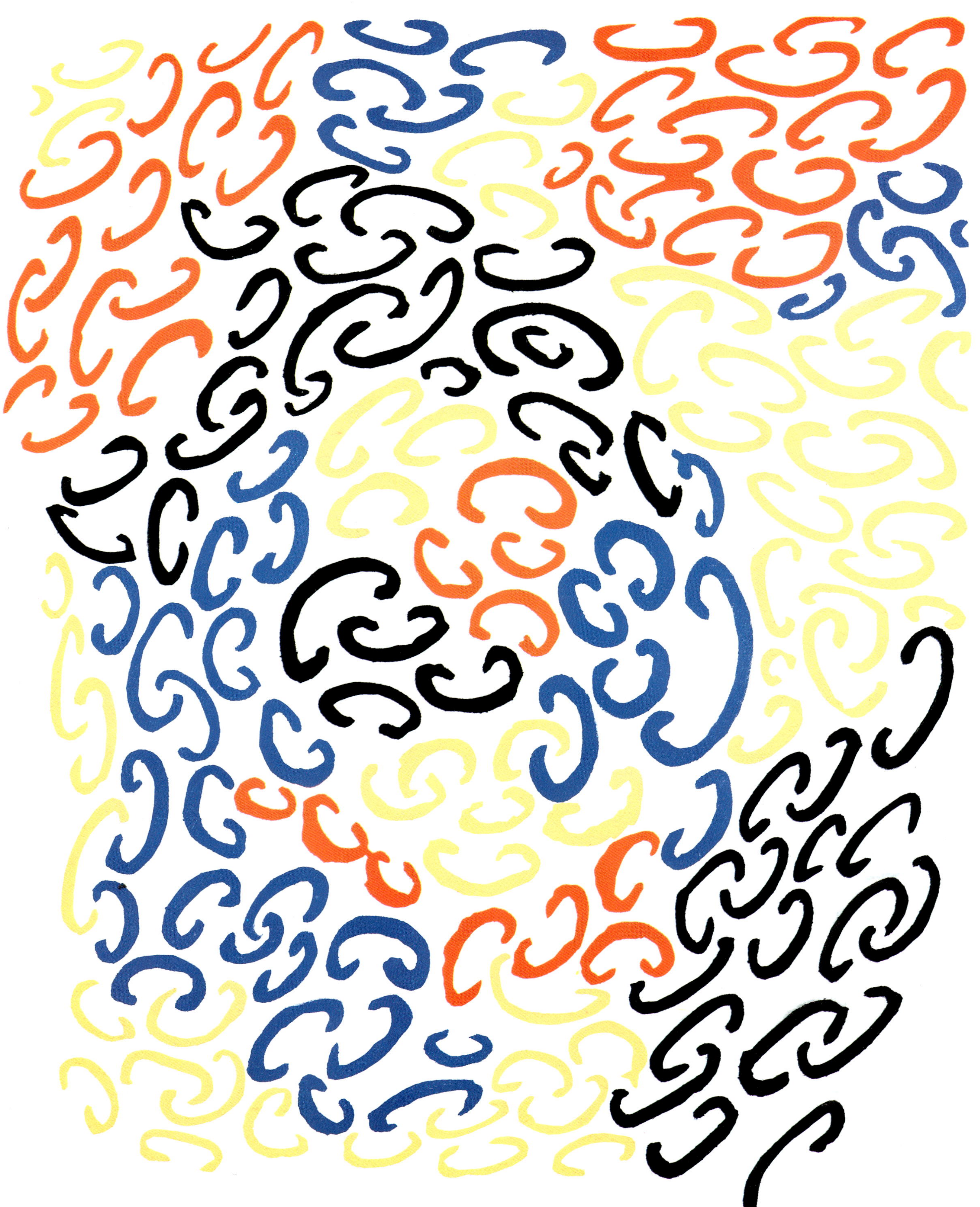

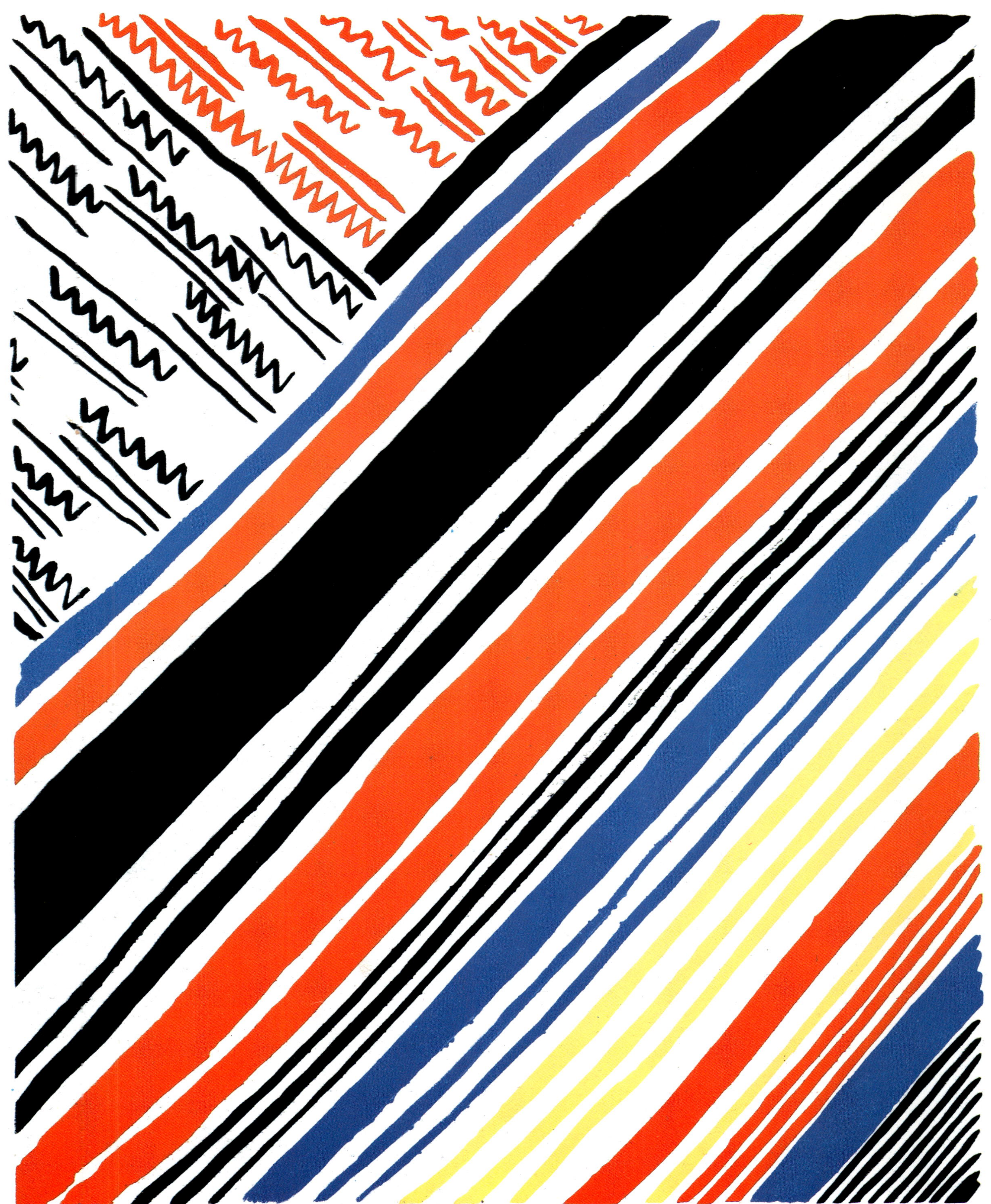

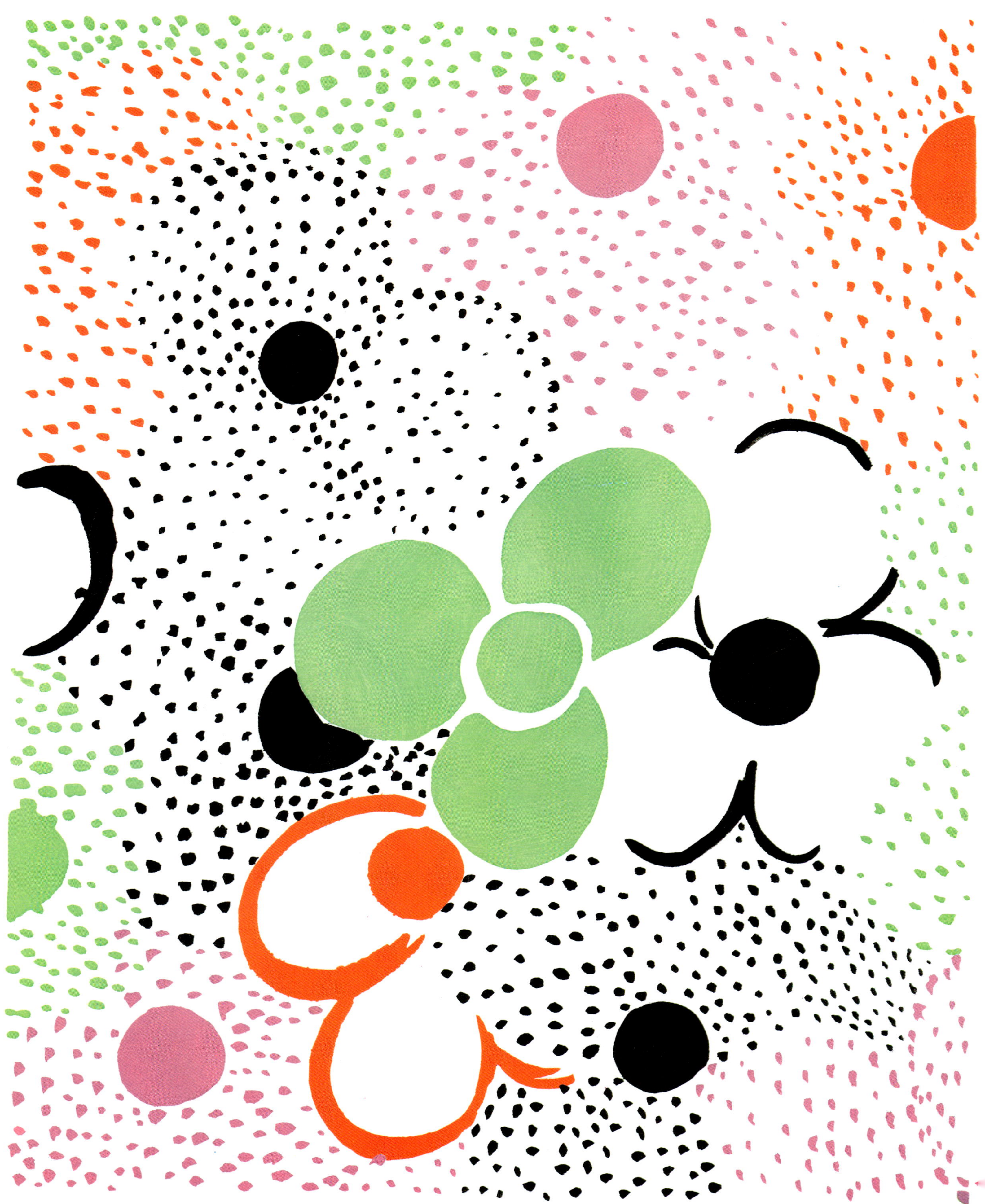

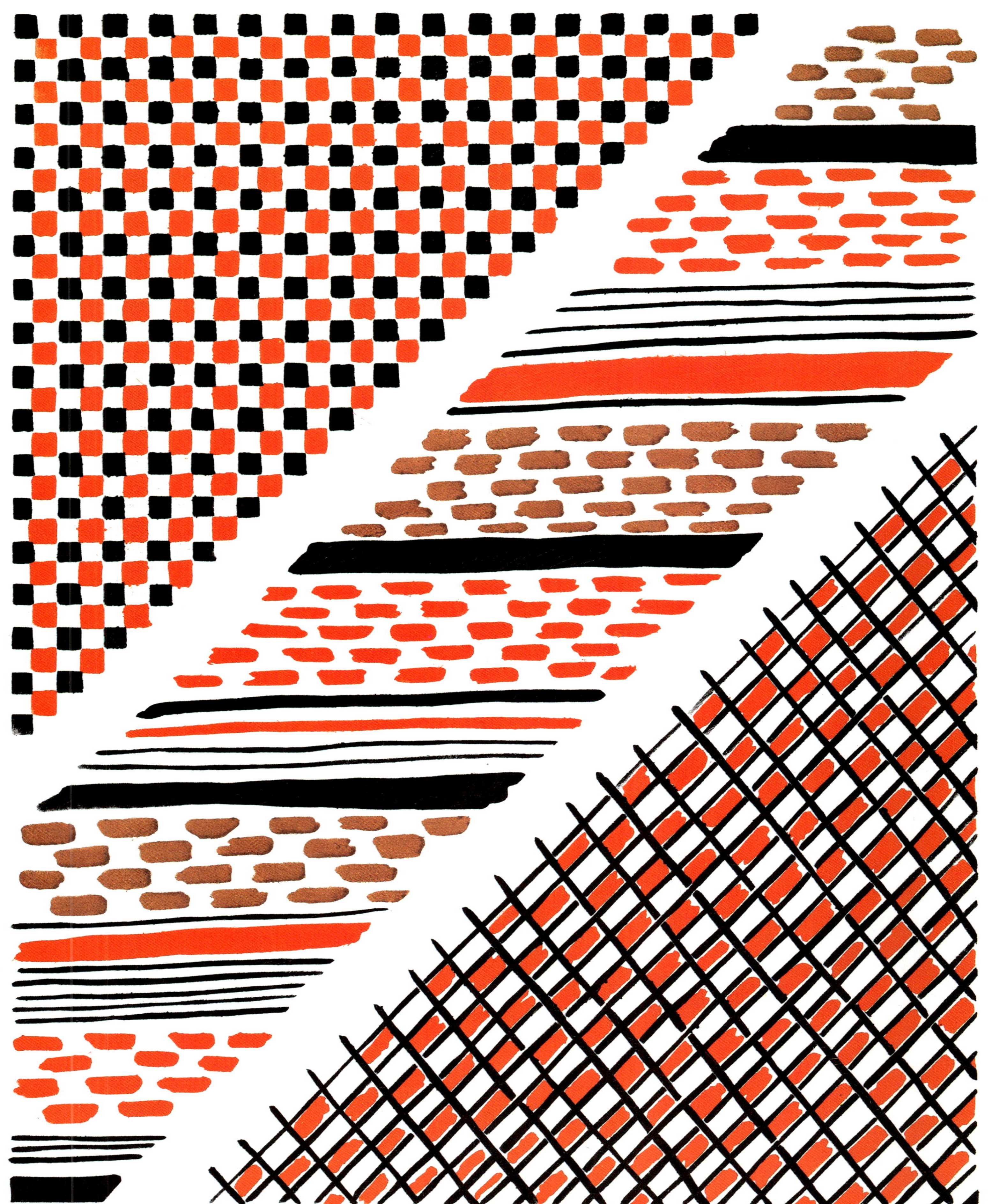

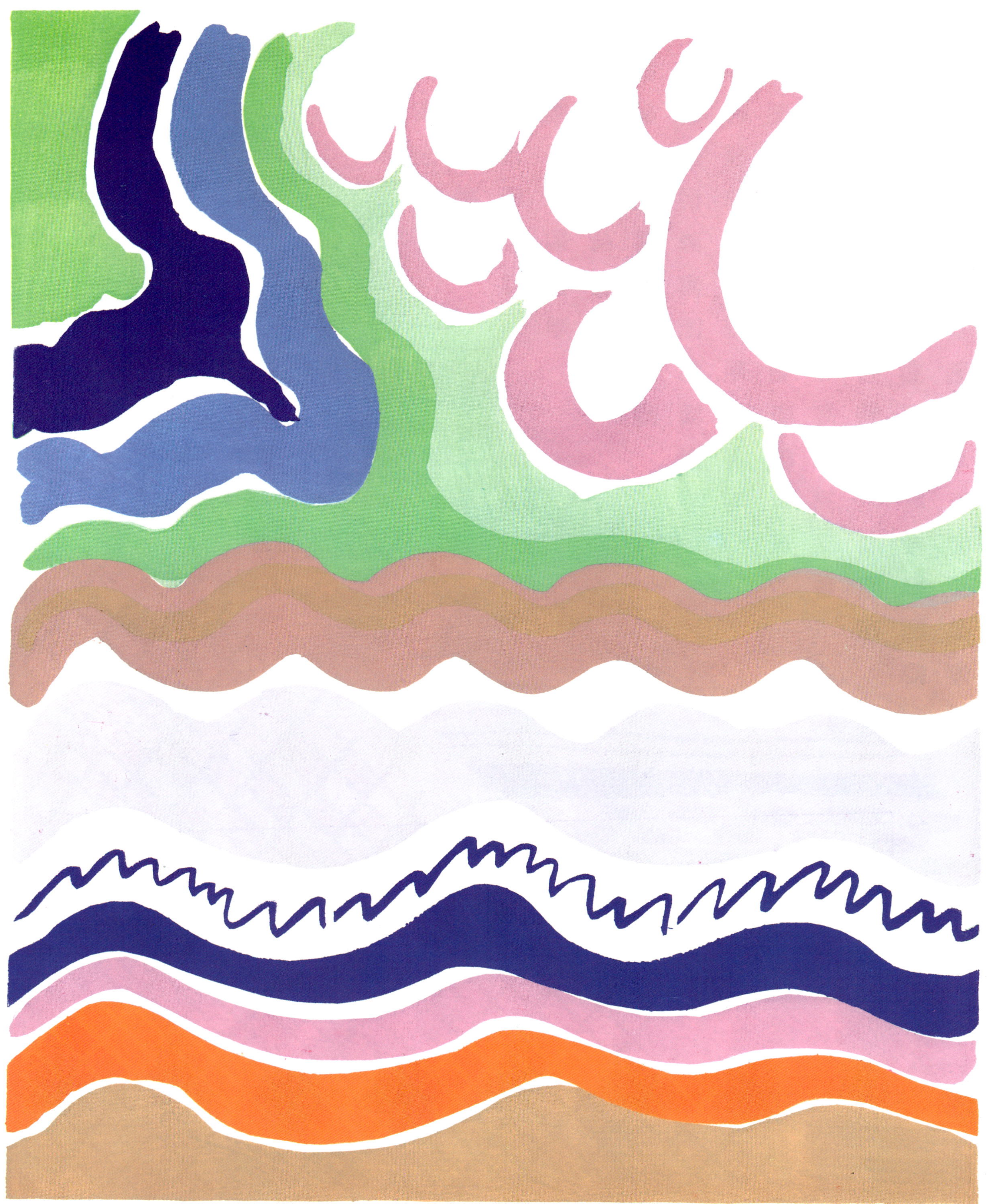

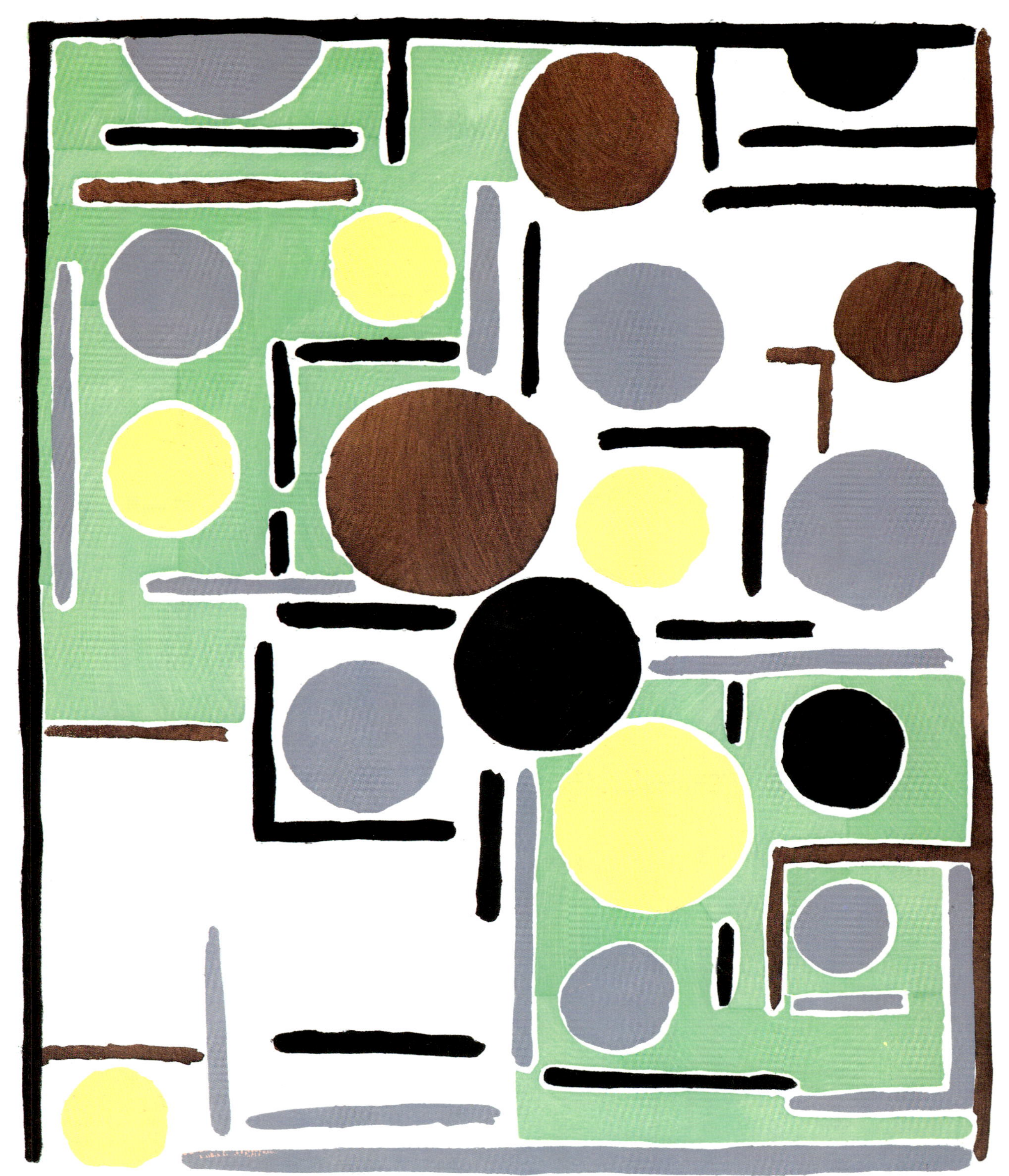

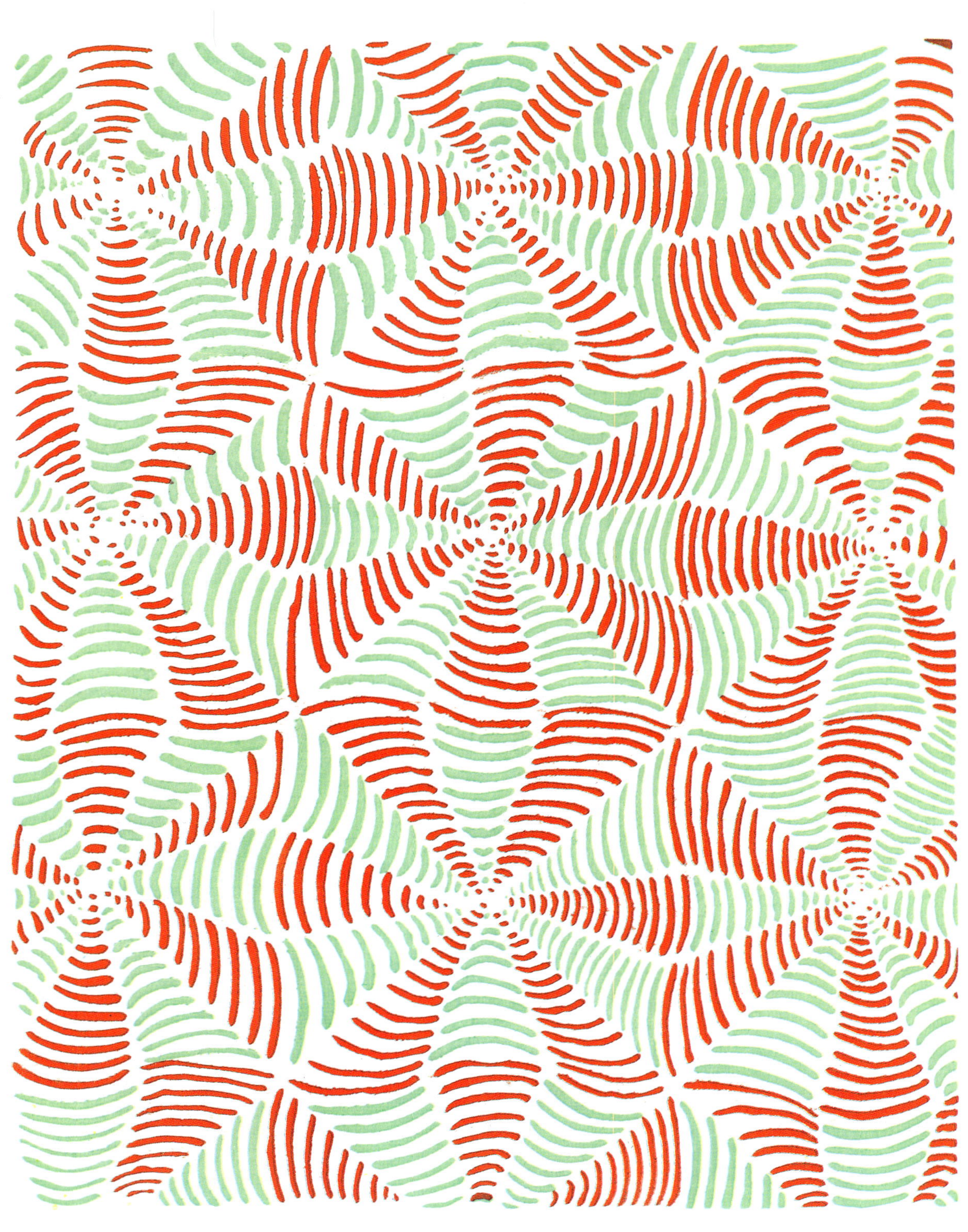

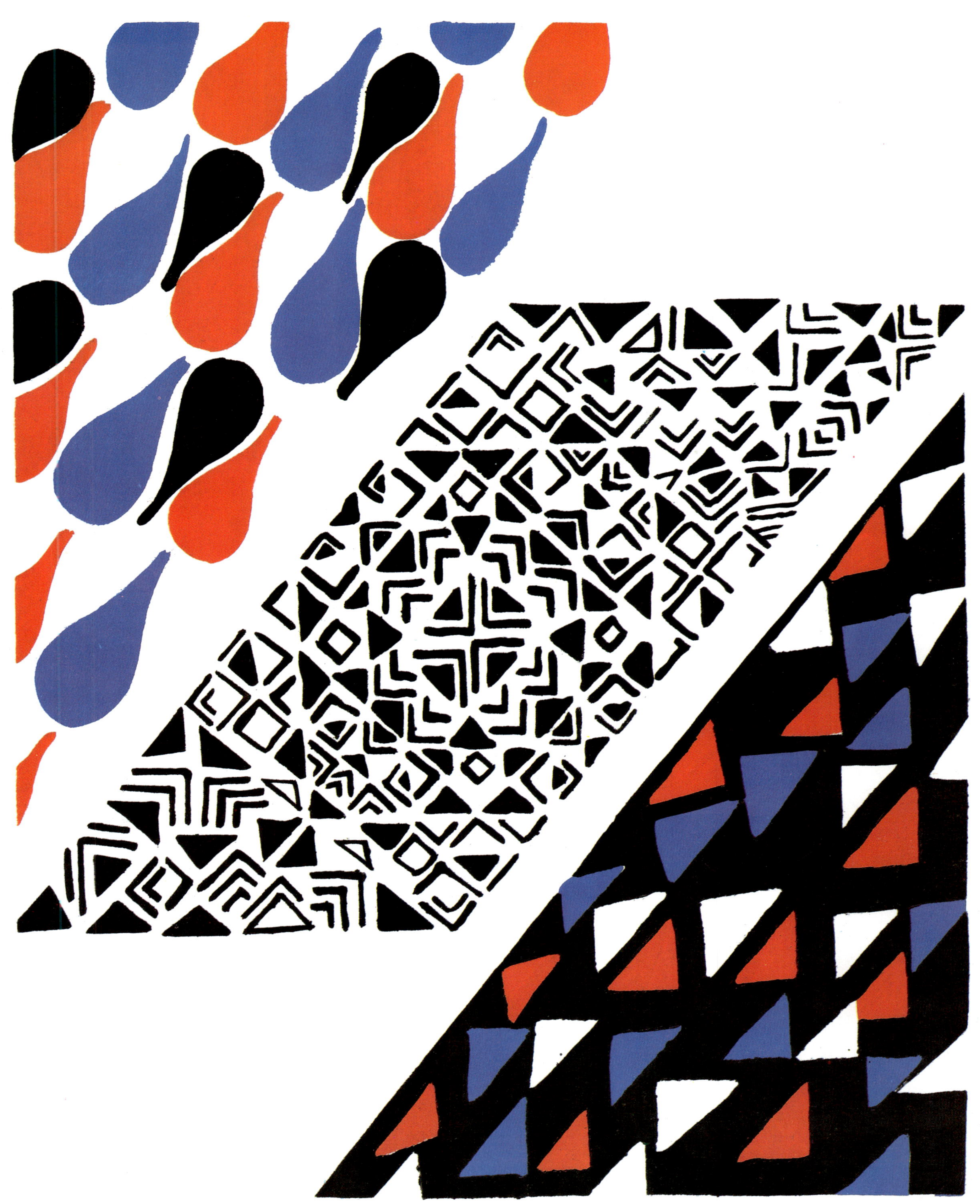

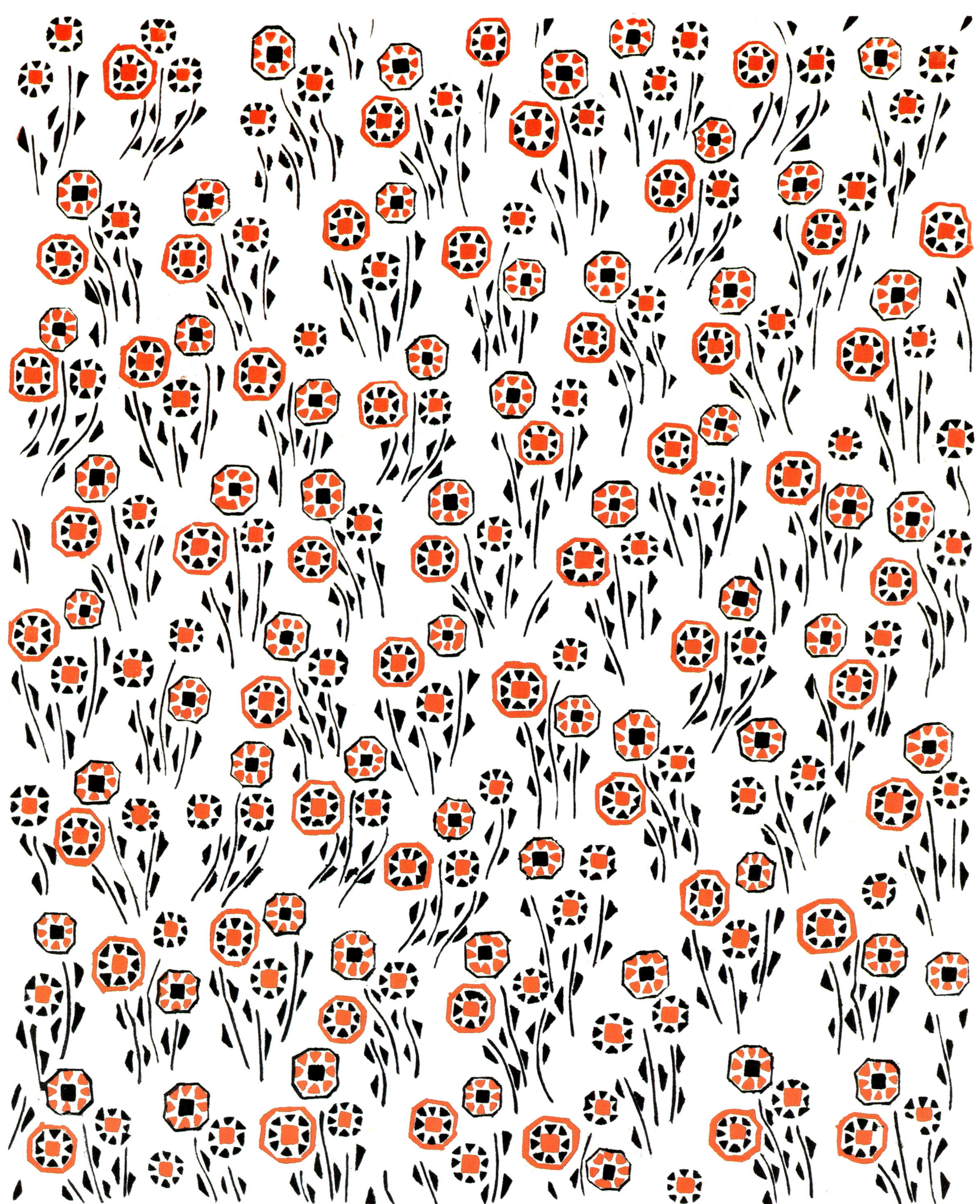

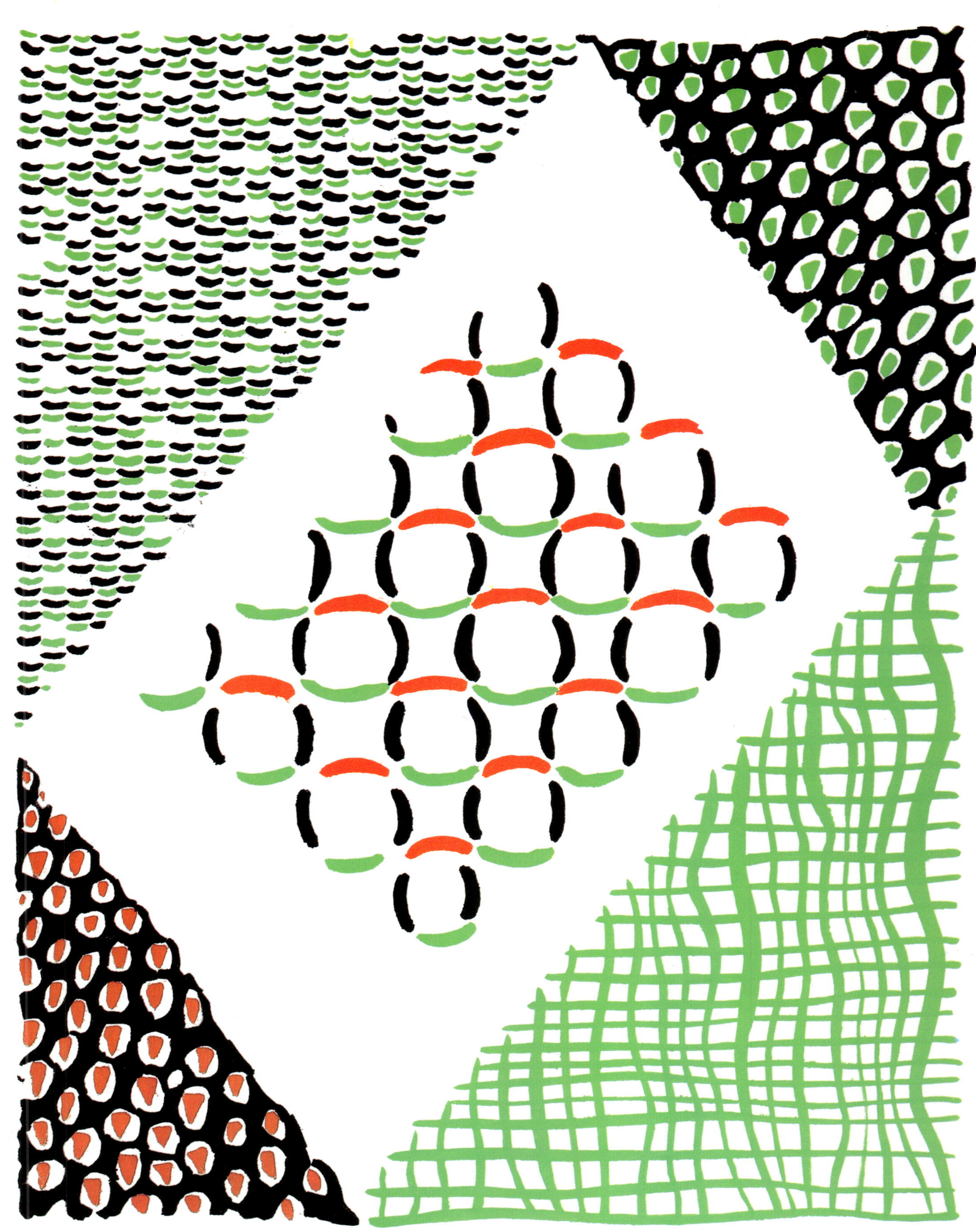

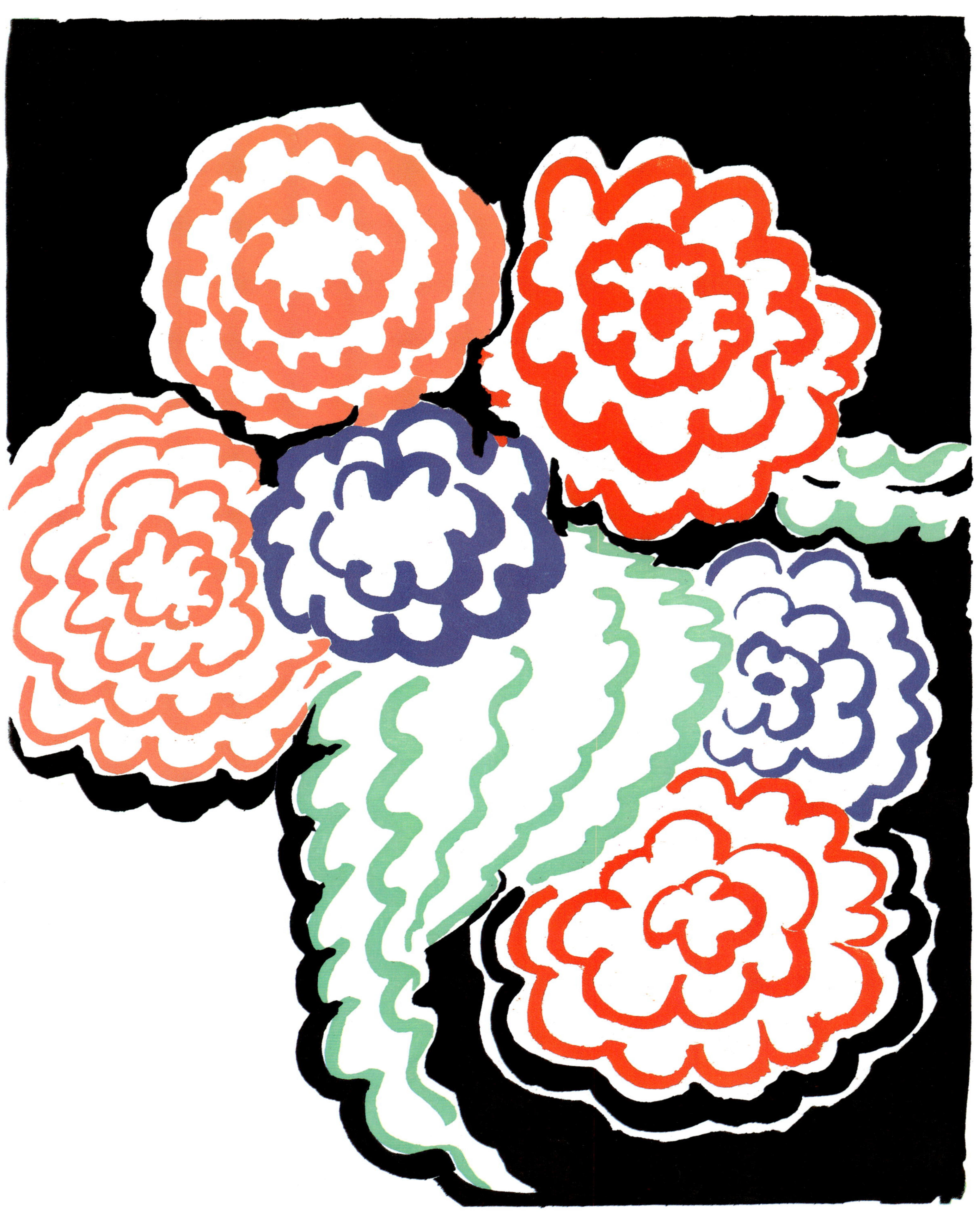

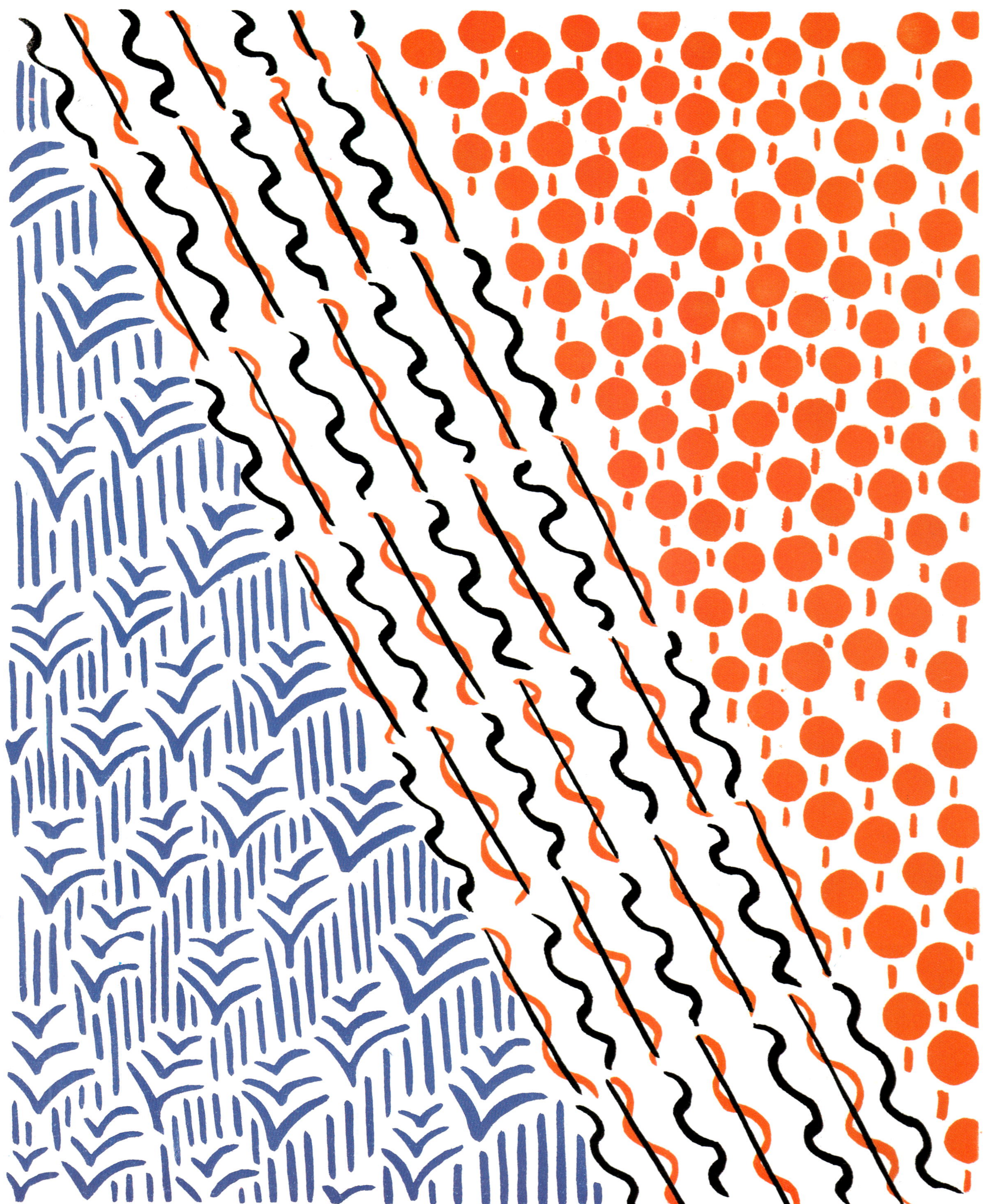

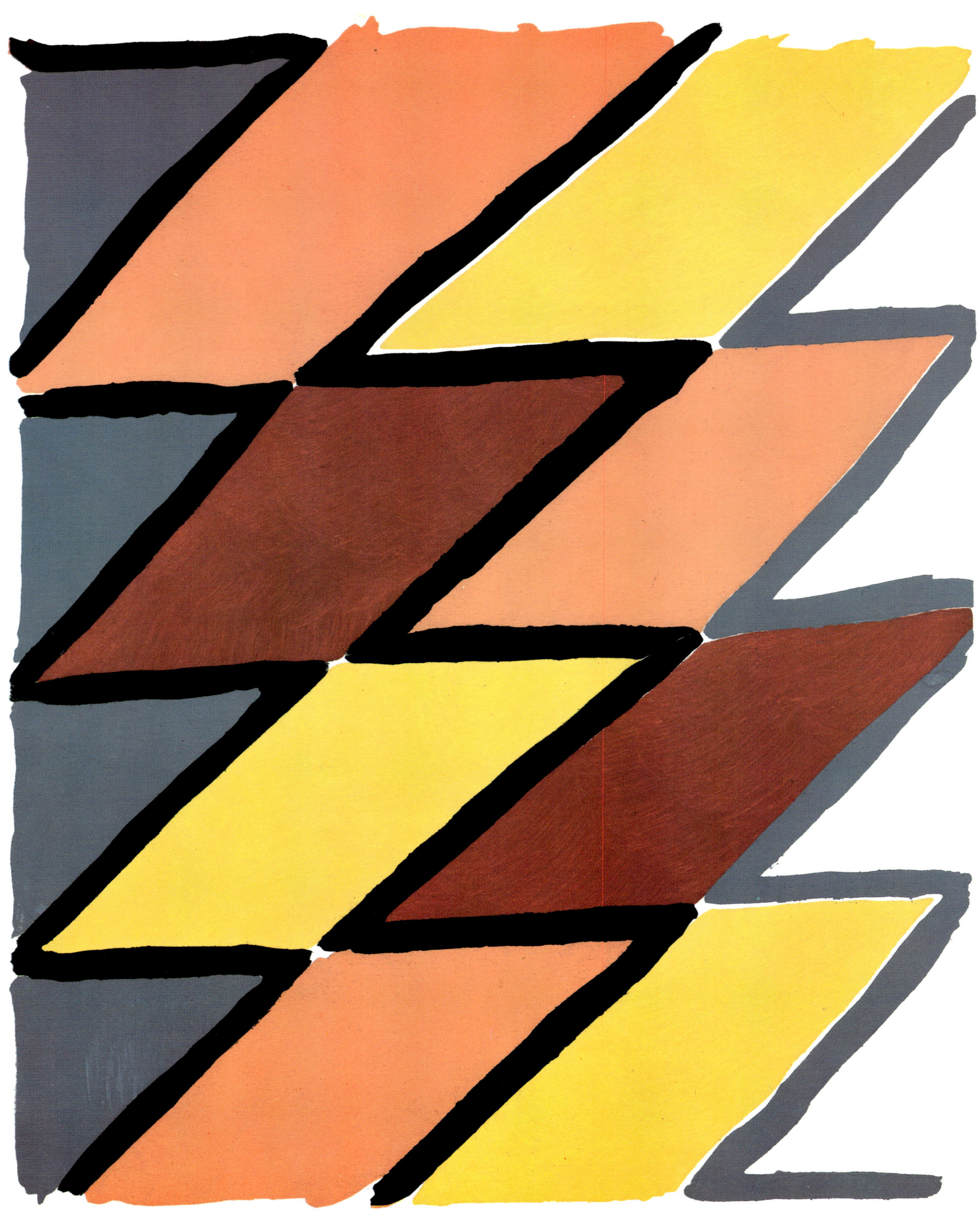

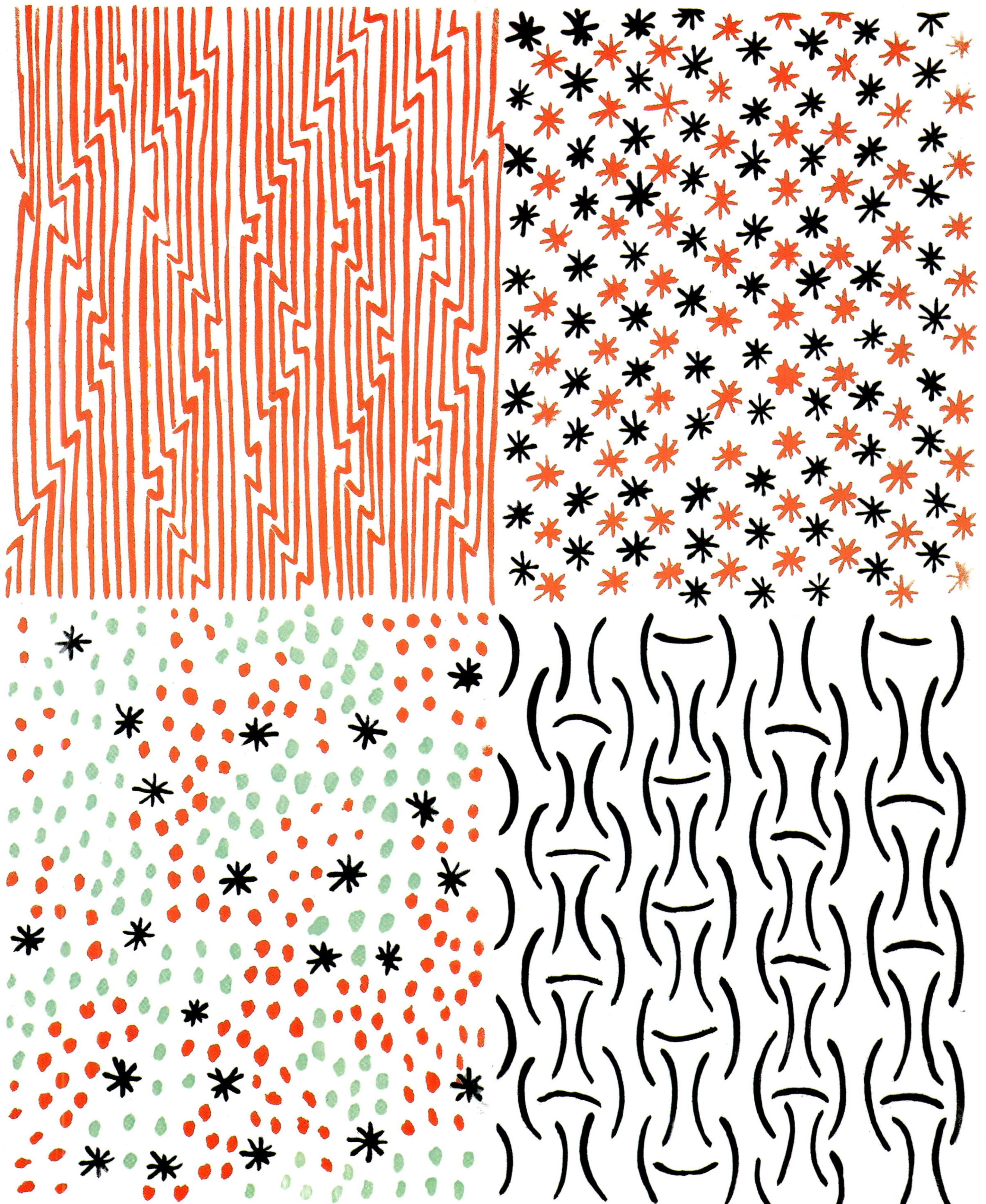

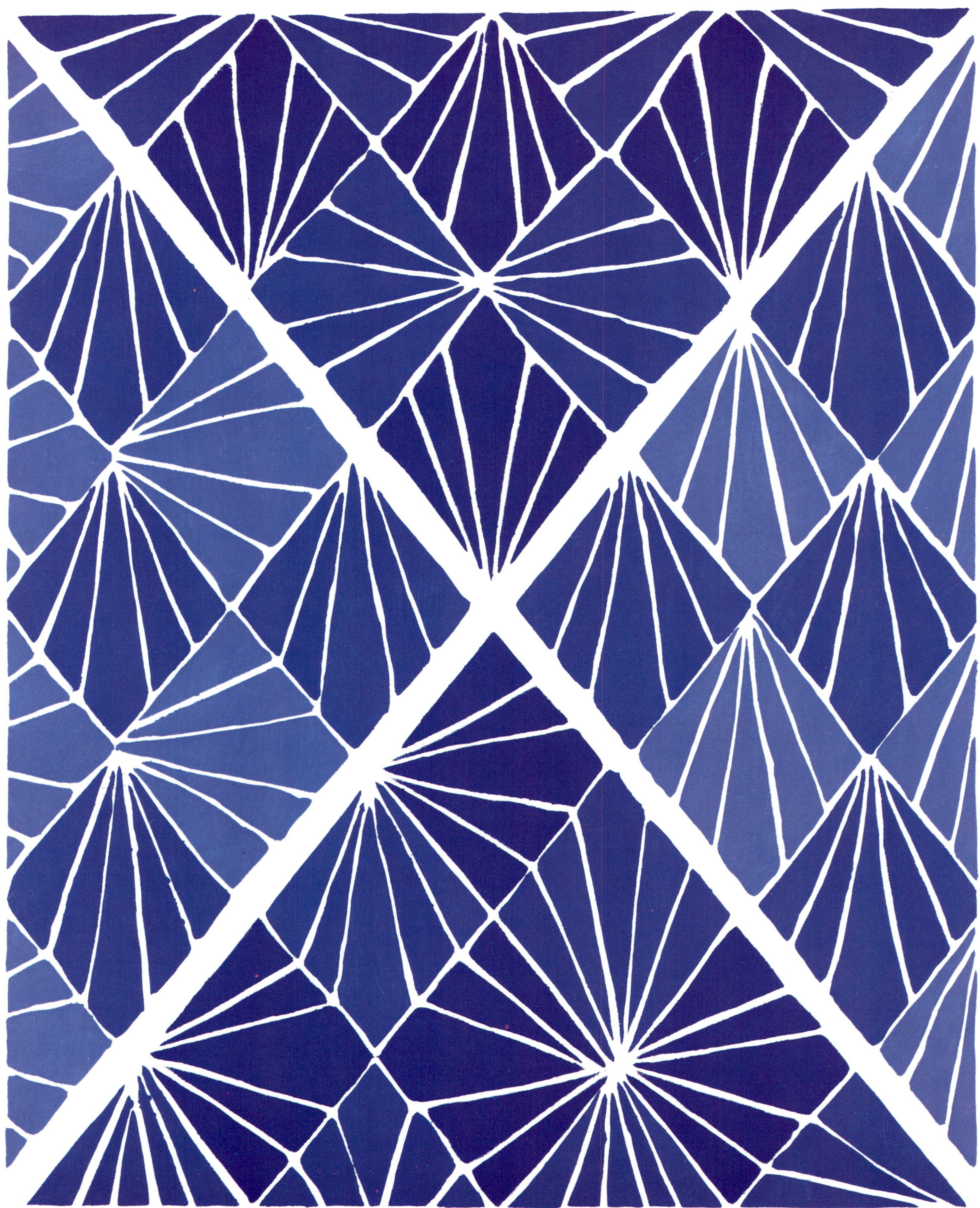

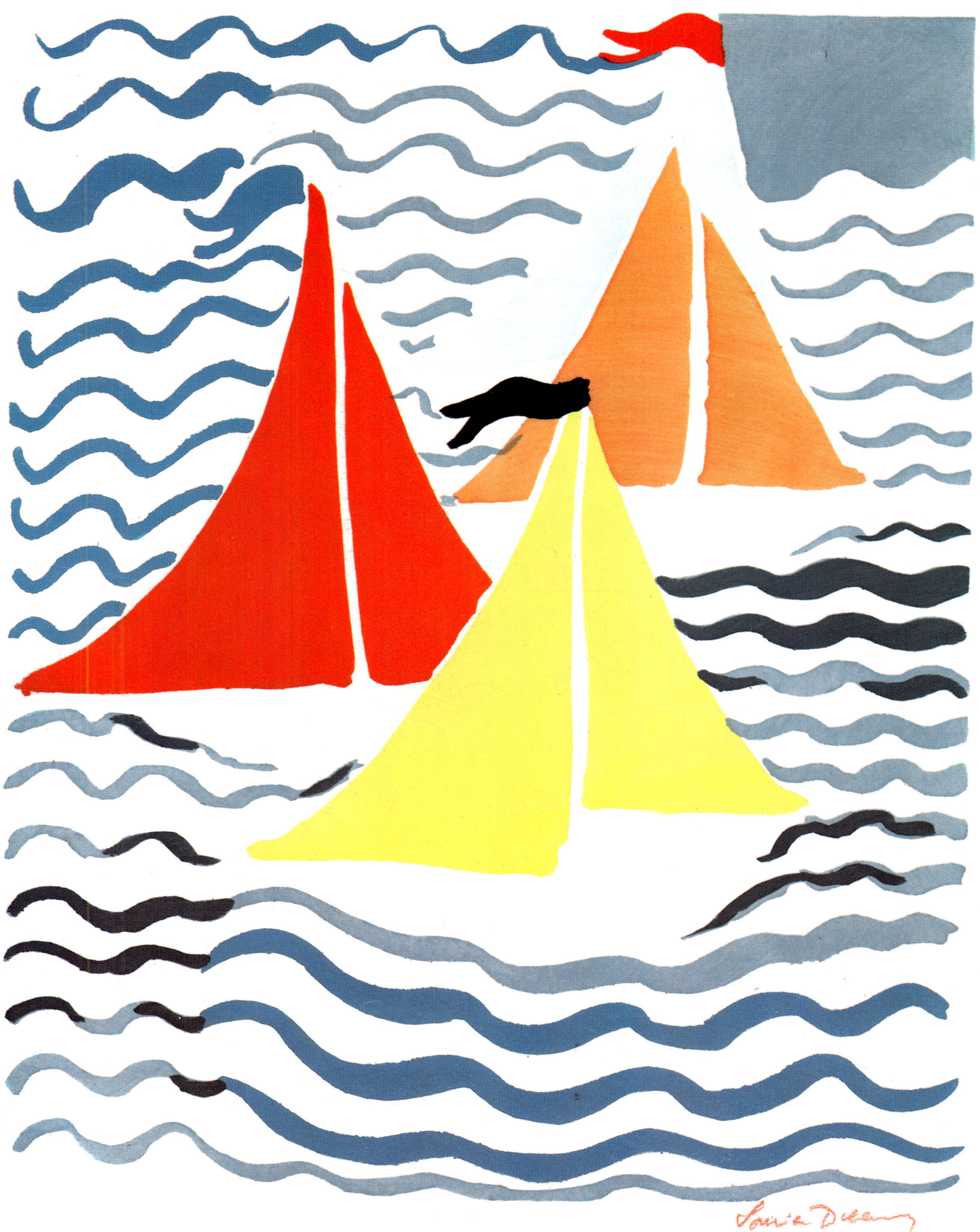

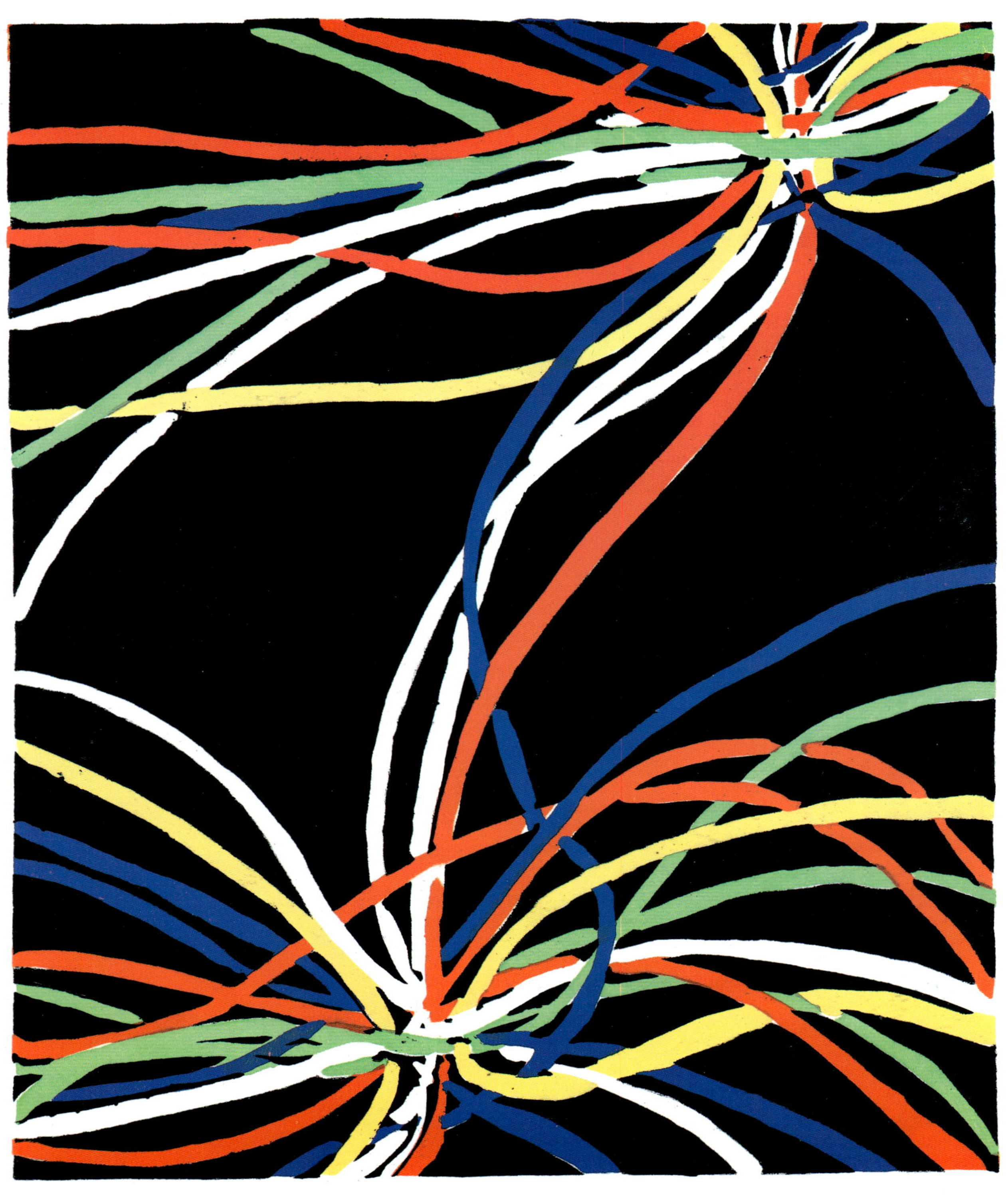

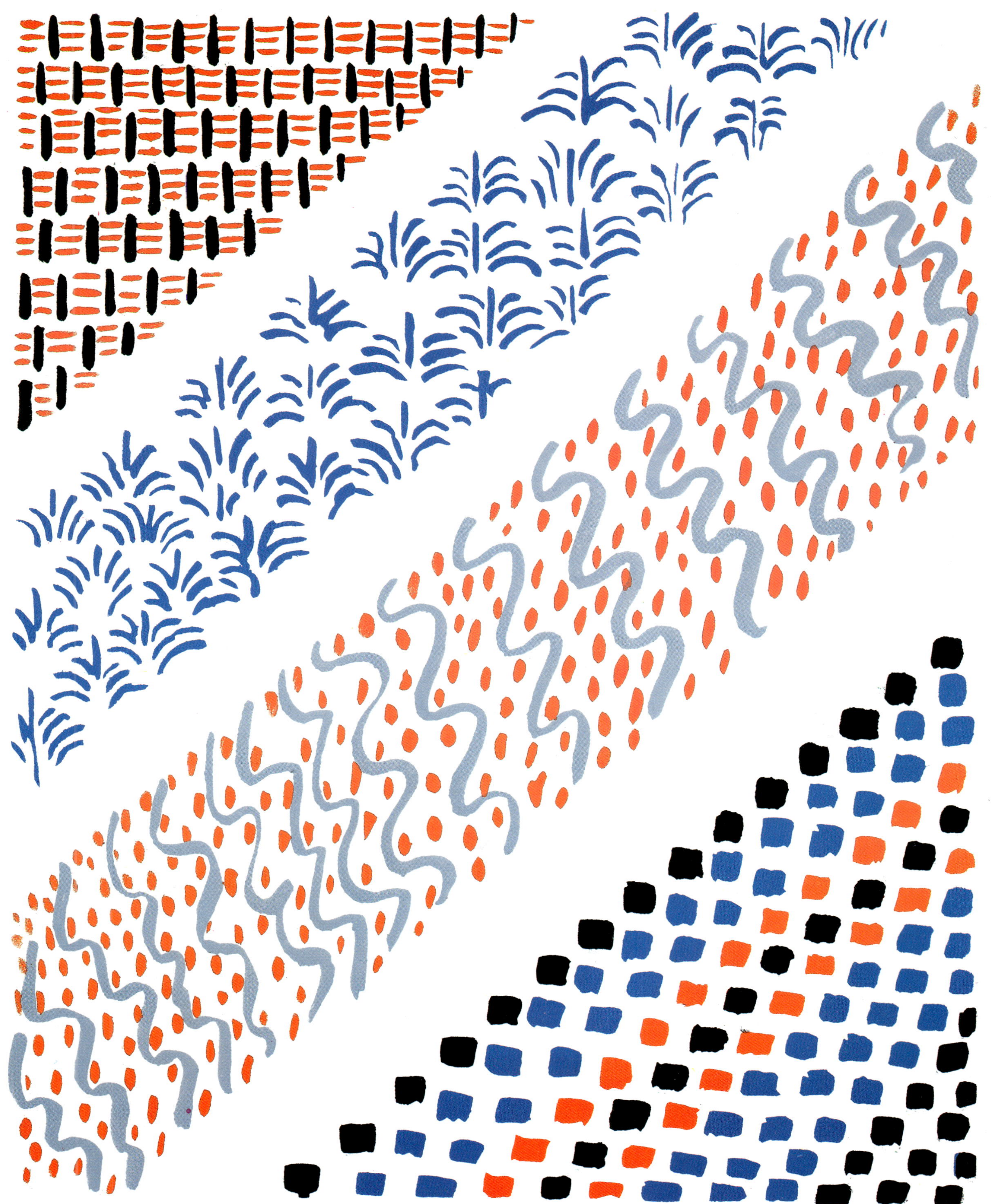

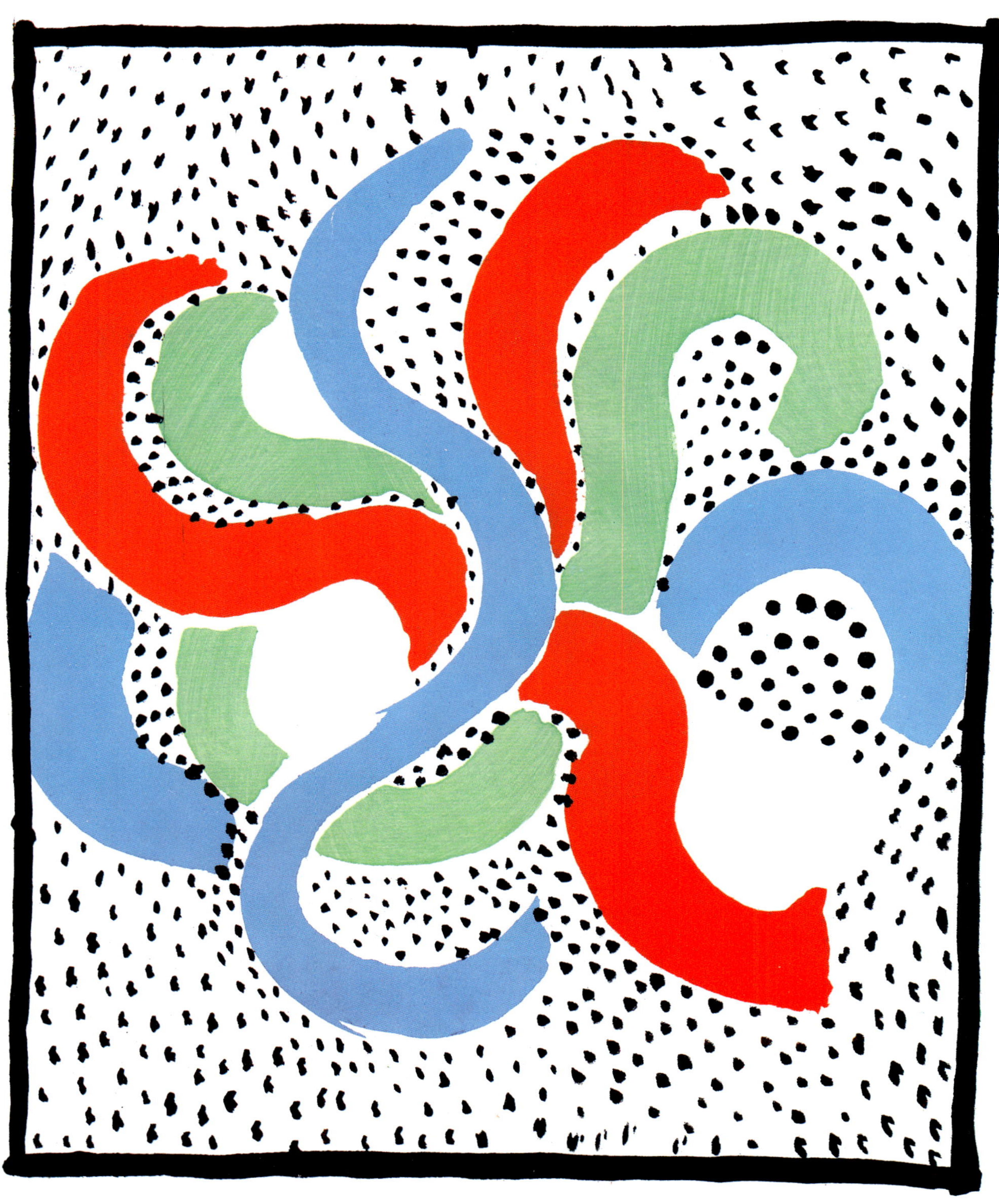

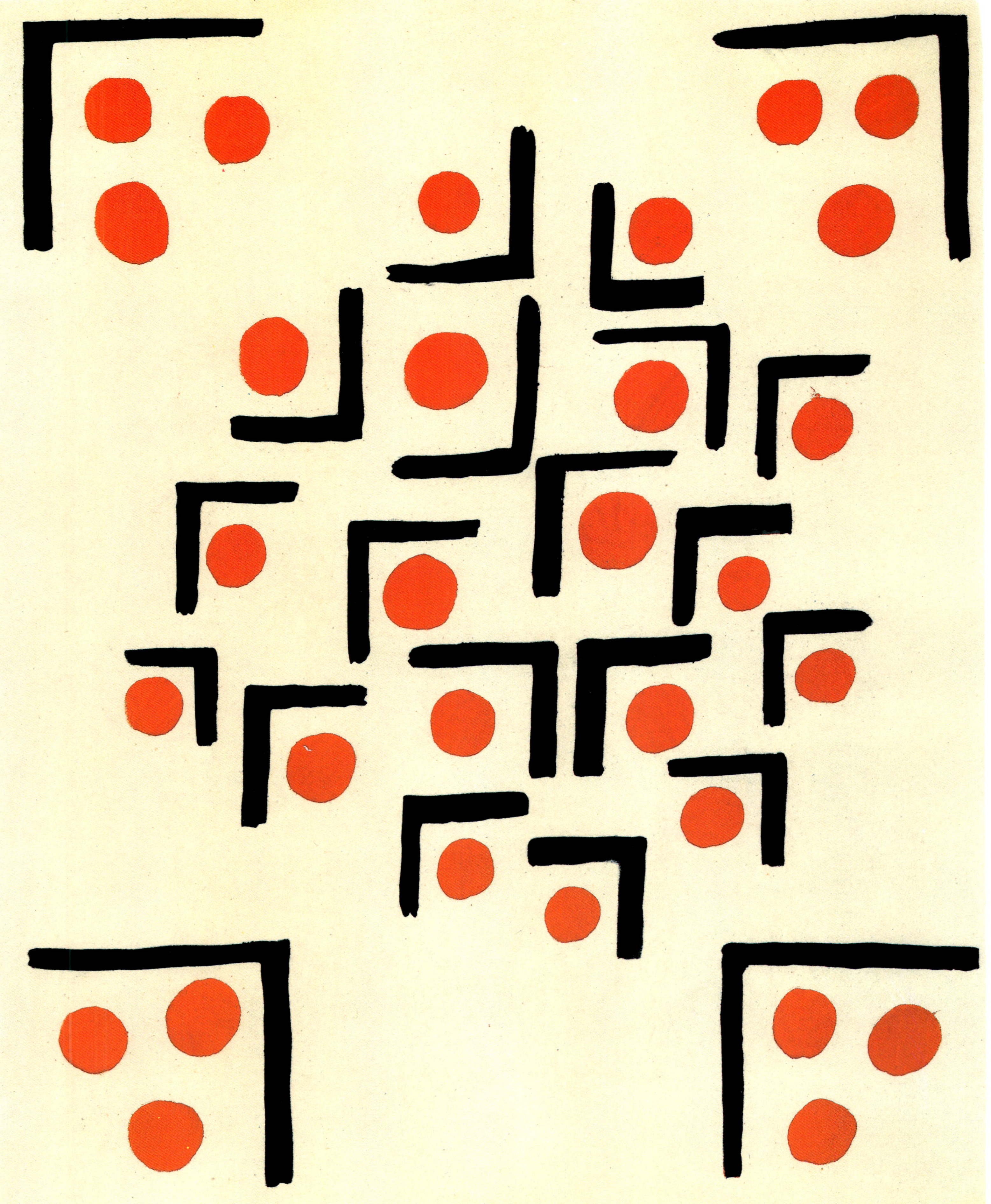

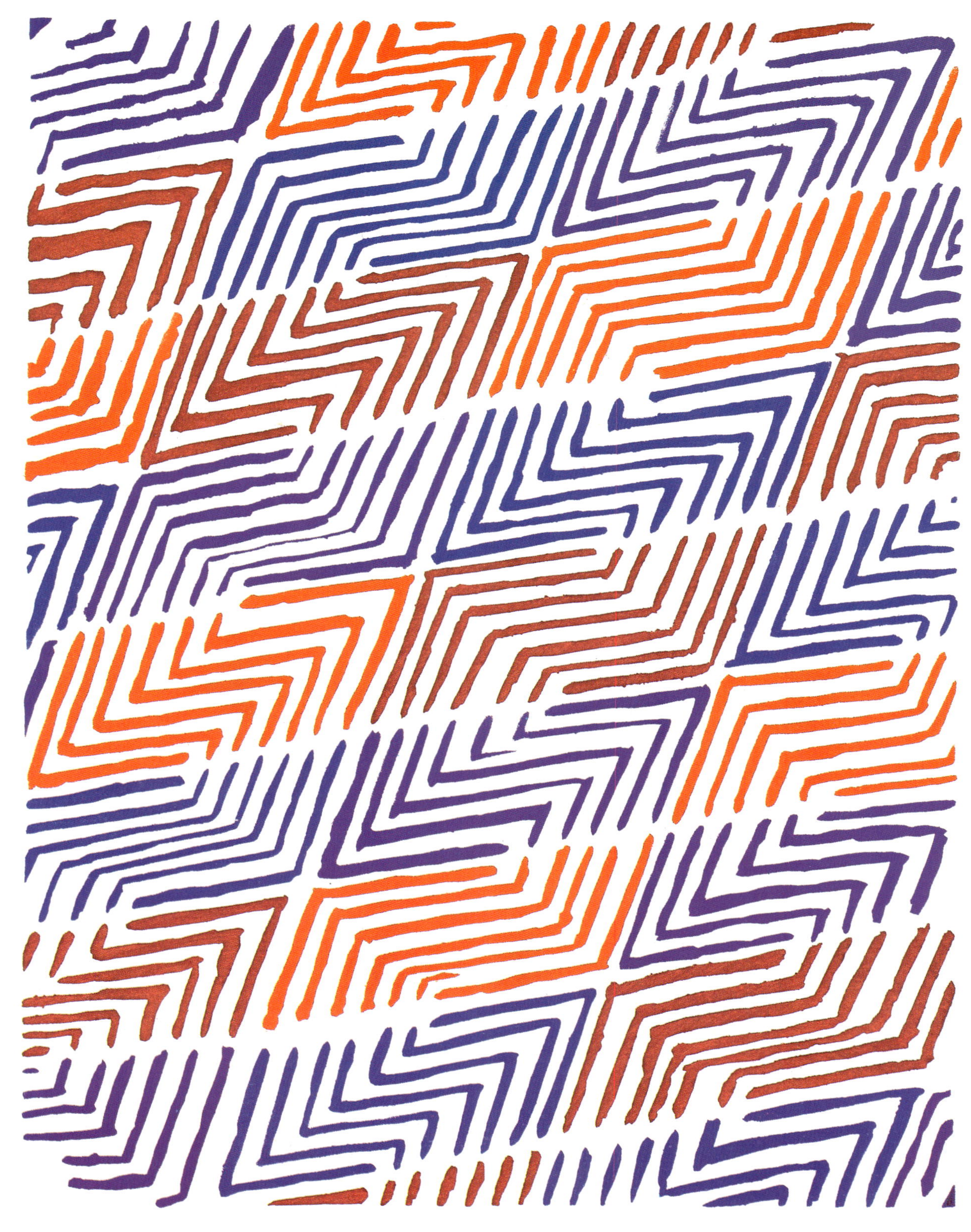

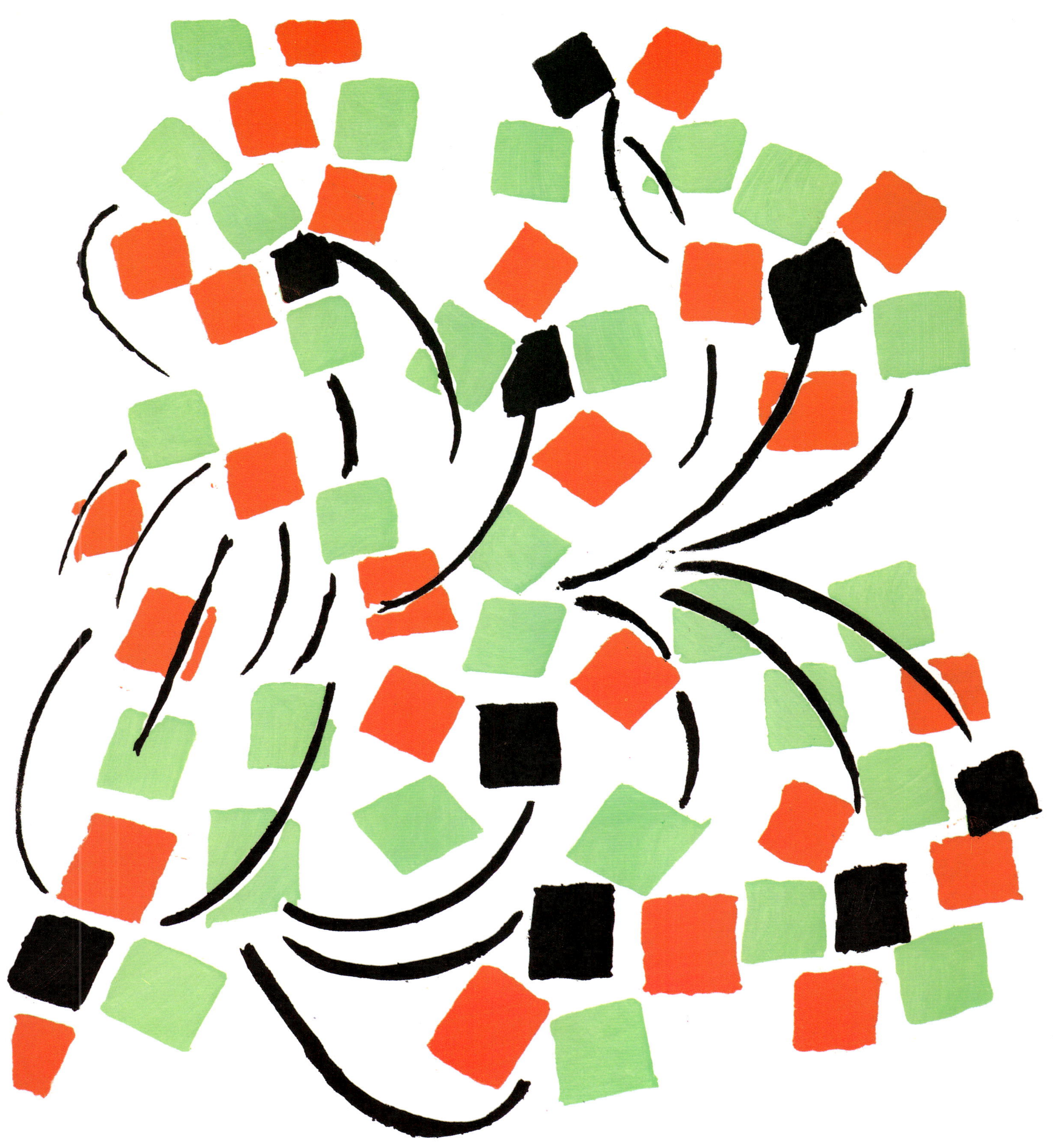

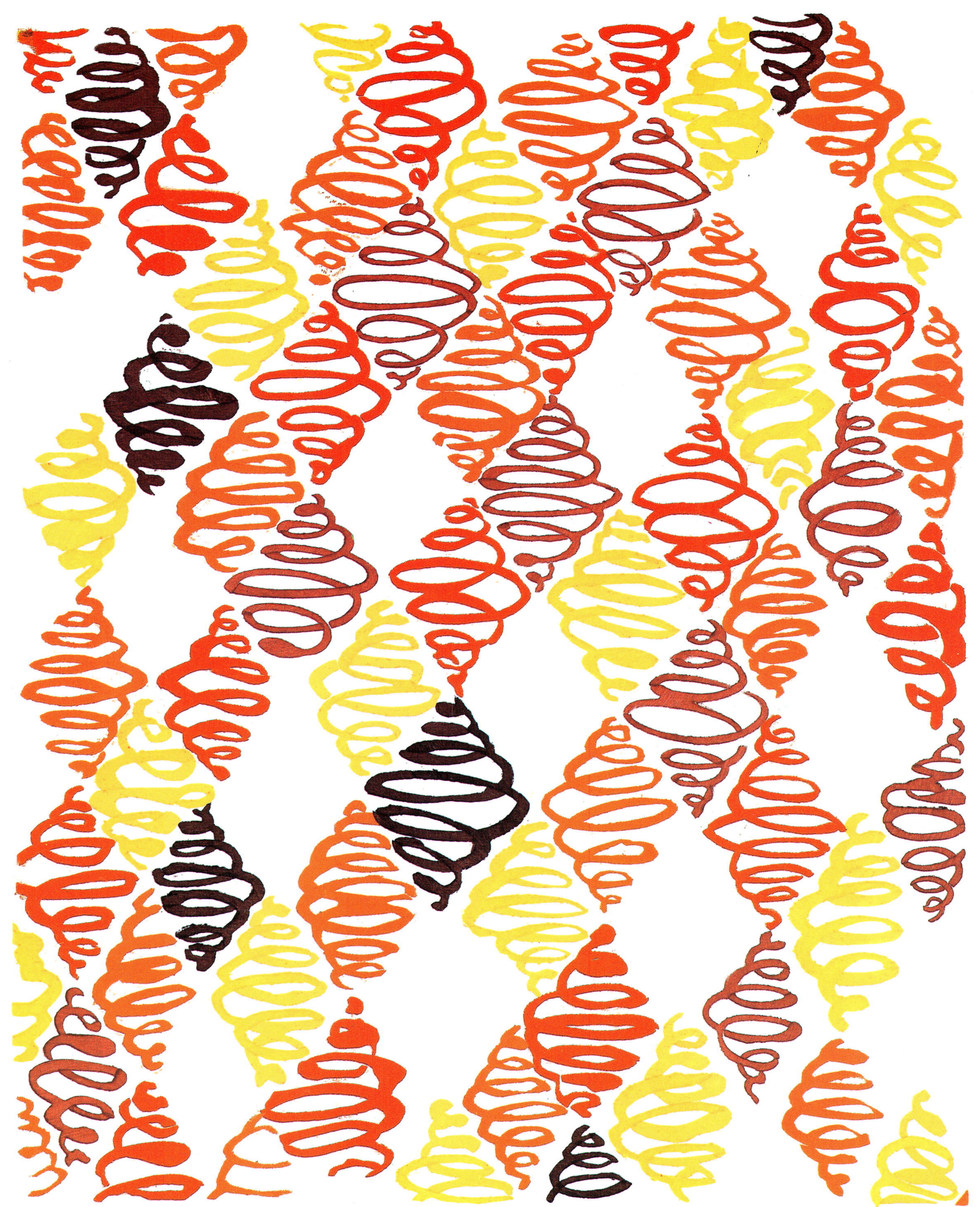

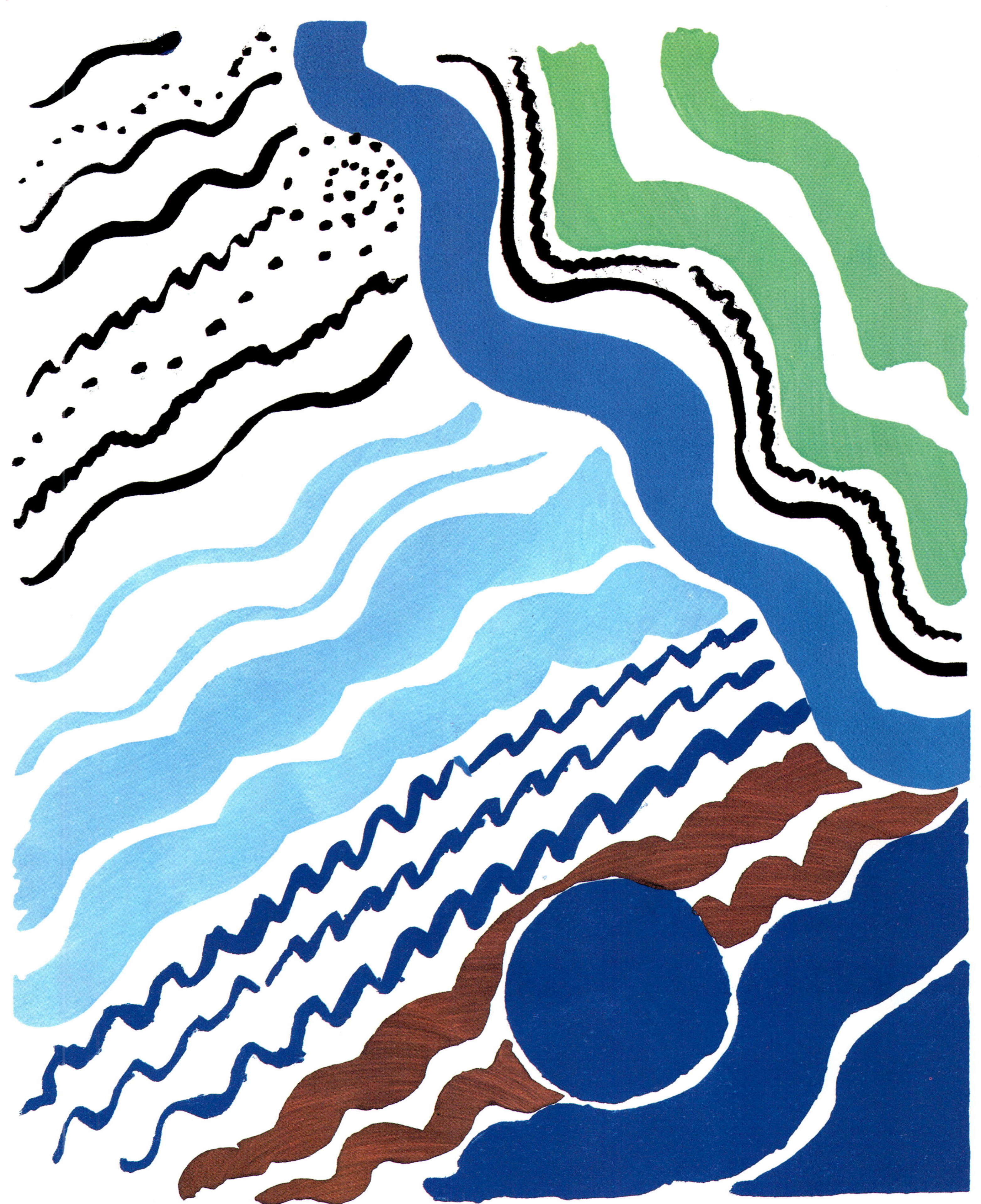

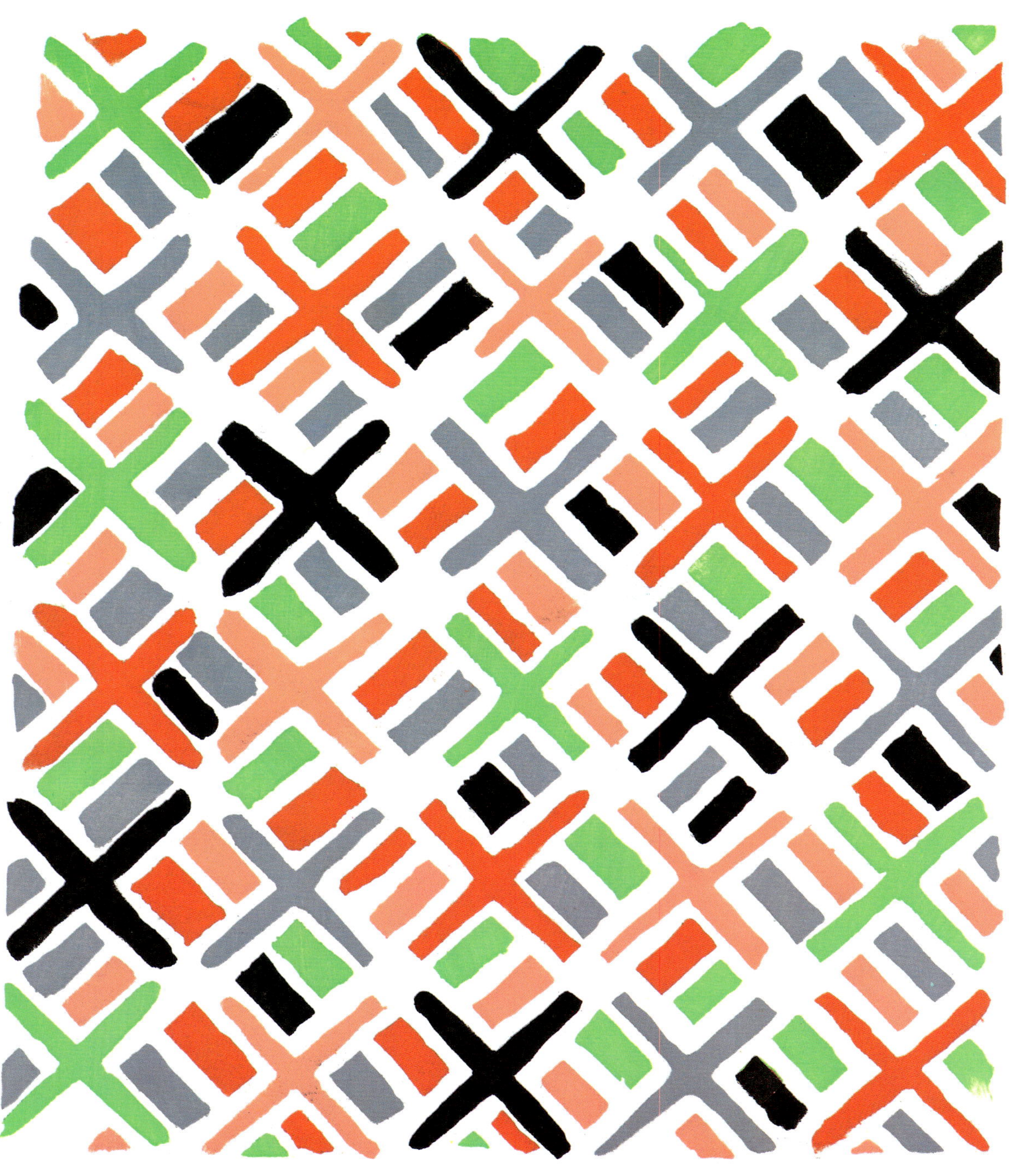

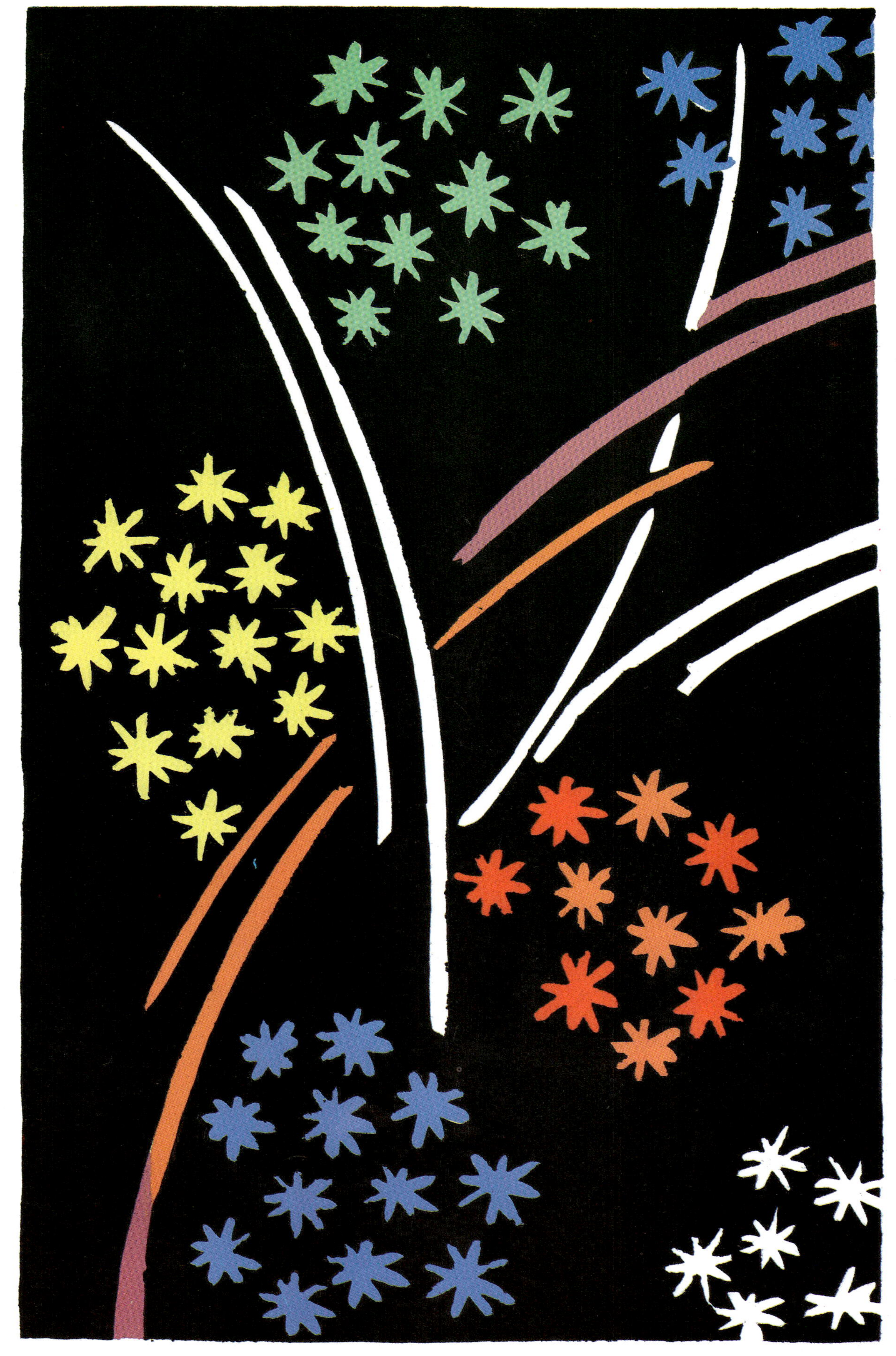

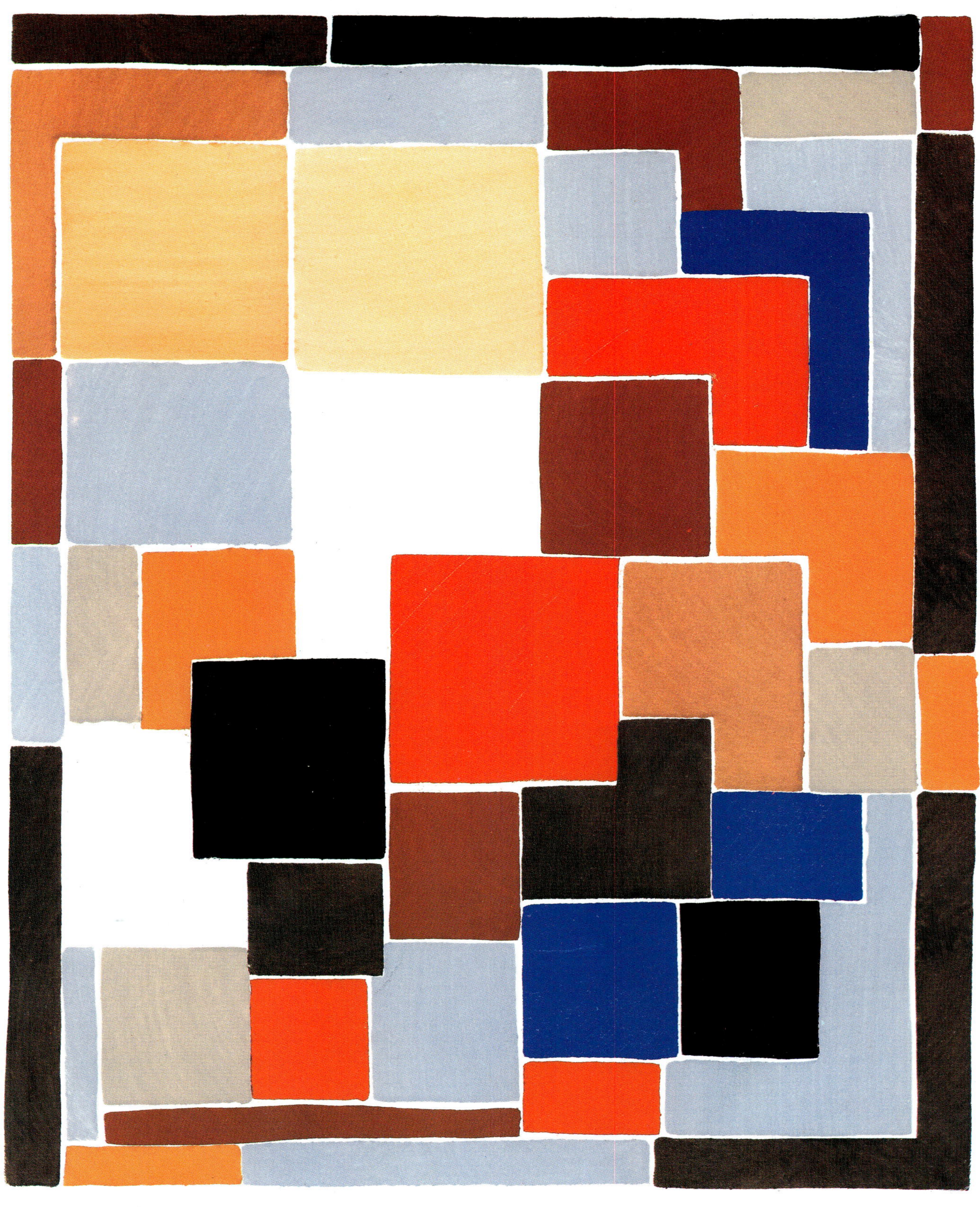

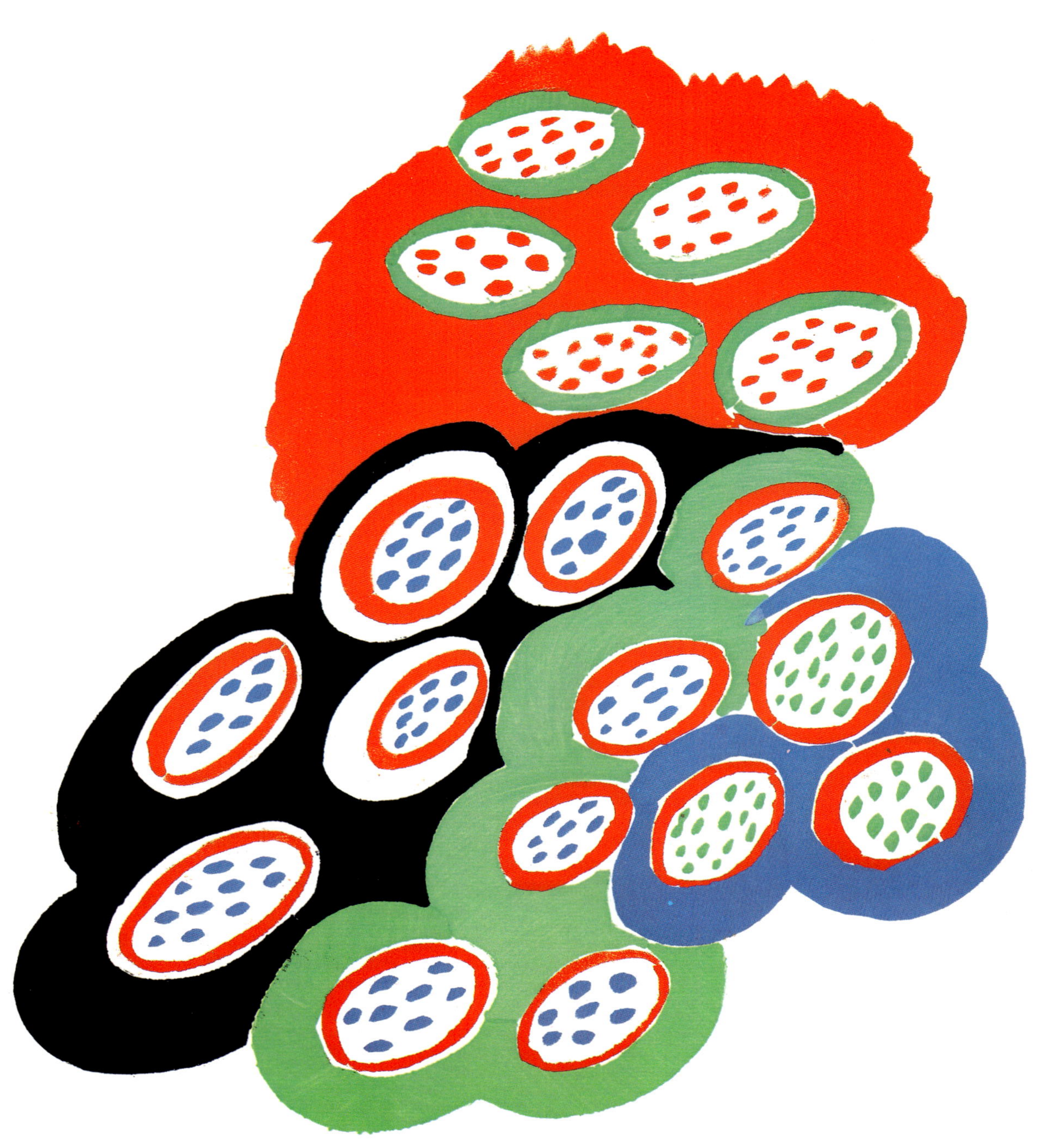

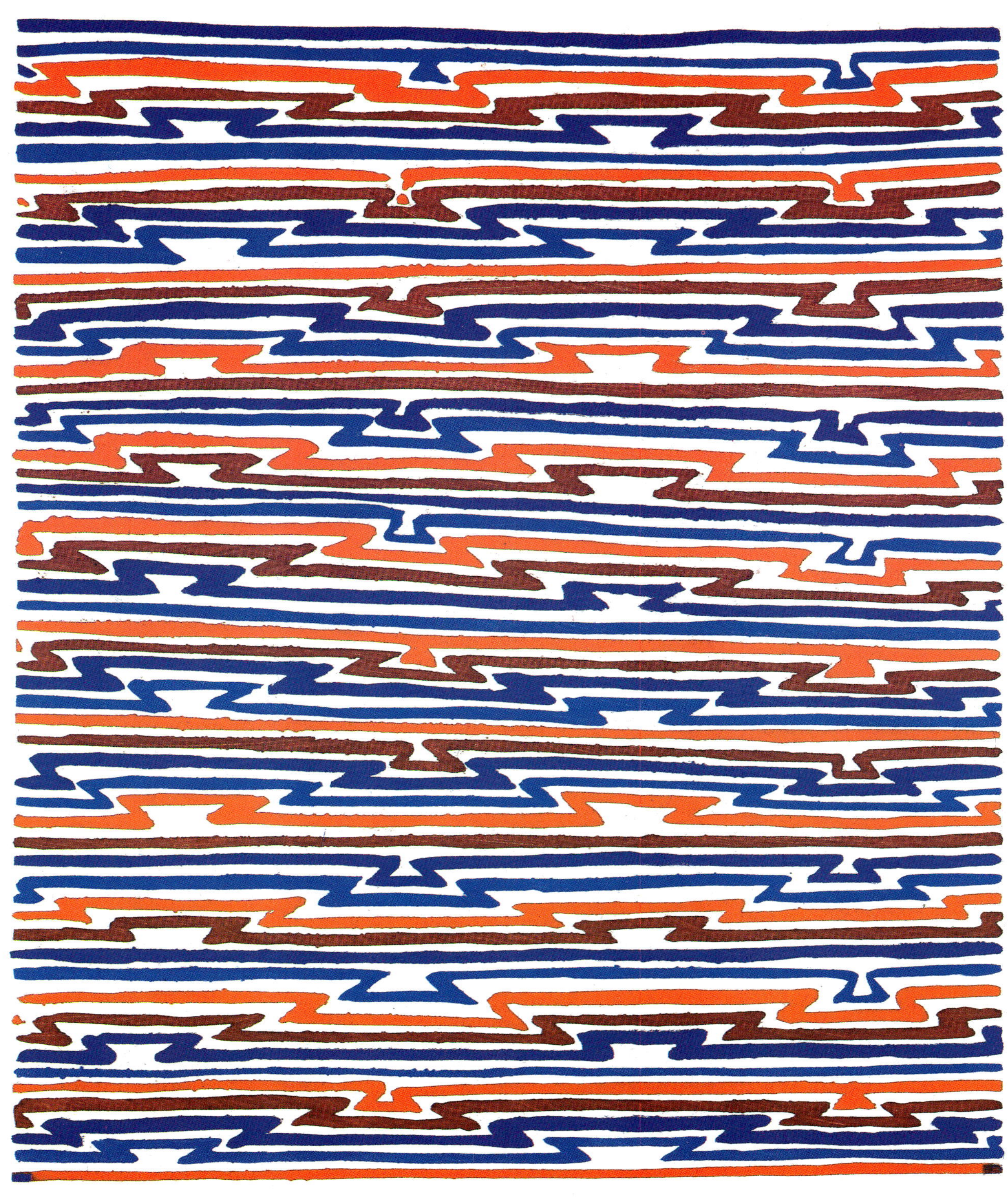

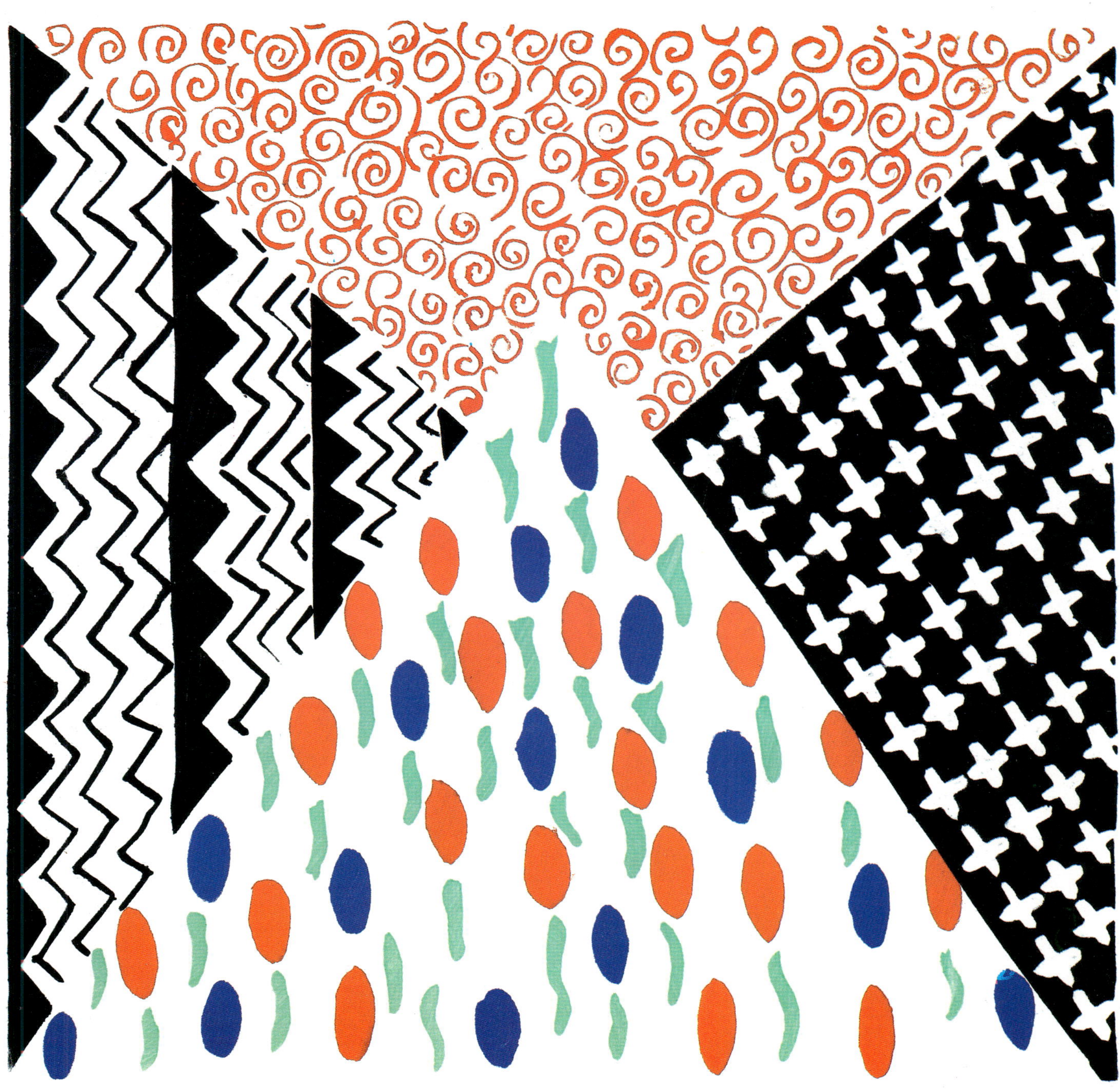

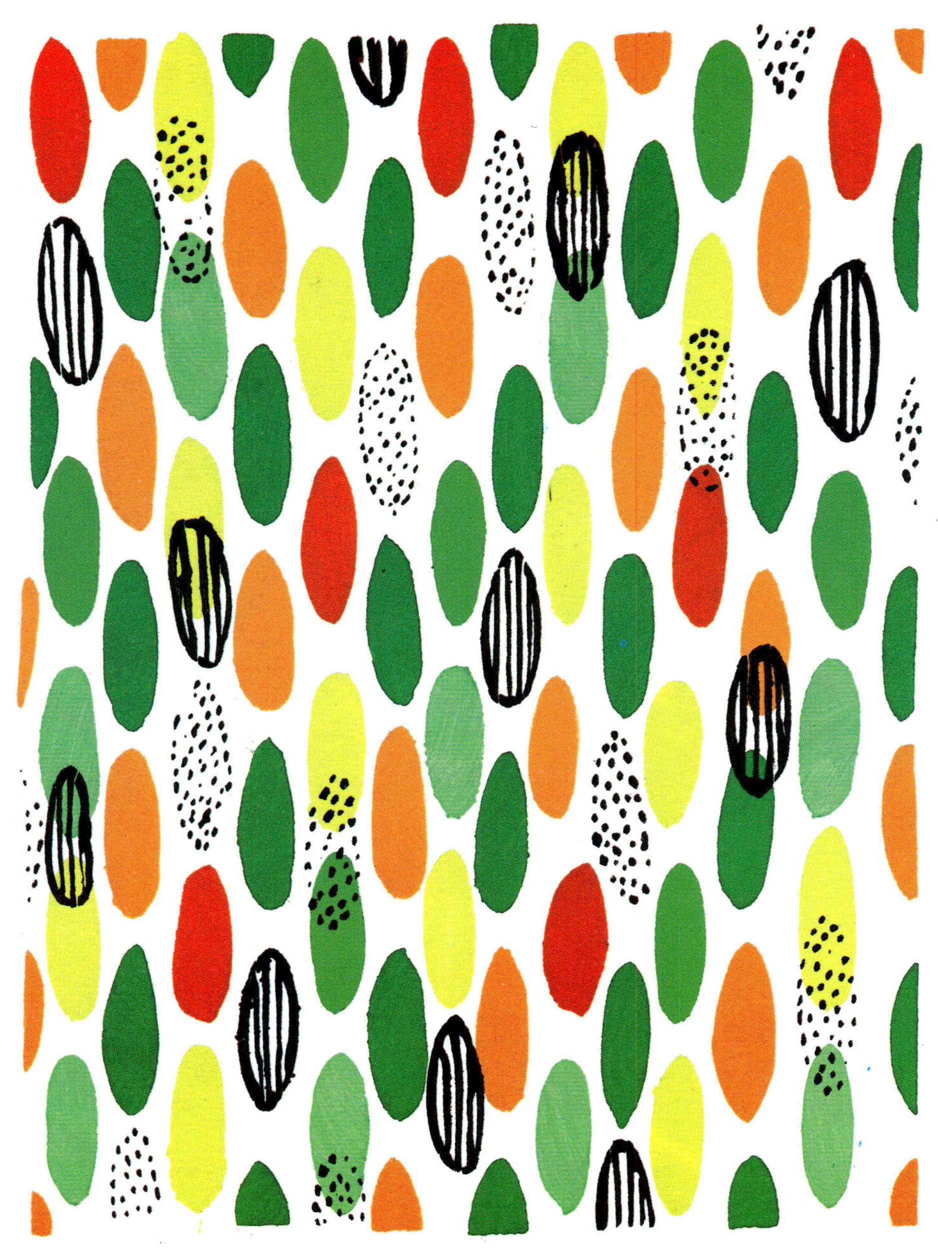